Praise for The Genesis of Creativity

The world is a better place when people express their creative ideas and solutions. God Himself is the Creator of creativity. Bil Hood has made a valuable contribution to our understanding of this mental process. From a biblical, research, and anecdotal perspective, his model shows how creativity works. He also provides practical action steps to develop our own. The book will help you find and live out your own God-given creativity.

John Townsend, Ph.D.
Psychologist, New York Times bestselling author of *Boundaries*, and founder of the Townsend Institute at Concordia University Irvine

As a leader with responsibilities in both the Church and the academy, I see clearly the need for resources that root human creativity in God's design. Hood's *Genesis of Creativity* does precisely this, showing how the opening chapters of Genesis frame our calling to cultivate, organize, and bring forth new possibilities in service to God and neighbor. This work reminds us that the creative impulse is not incidental but part of the Creator's own gift woven into humanity from the beginning. For Christians tasked with guiding institutions, shaping culture, or nurturing faithful imagination, Hood provides a steady and Scripture-rich guide that bridges theology and practice with uncommon clarity.

Dr. Michael Thomas, President
Concordia University Irvine

In The Genesis of Creativity, Bil Hood offers a thoughtful and inspiring exploration of creativity as a gift rooted in the very character of God. This book echoes an essential truth: we are created in the image of a God who creates, sustains, and renews. Hood skillfully weaves together biblical foundations, contemporary research, and engaging real-life stories to show that creativity is not a niche talent reserved for a few, but a God-given capacity designed for all people. Hood encourages readers to recognize their creative abilities as gifts entrusted by God for the building up of others and the flourishing of the world. Insightful, accessible, and richly grounded in Scripture, The Genesis of Creativity invites readers to discover and confidently use their God-given creative potential. It is a meaningful resource for anyone seeking to understand creativity not merely as a human skill, but as a reflection of God's ongoing creative work in and through His people.

Dr. Leslie A. Smith
Educational Leadership Consultant; Training and Development Specialist, Keynote Speaker

This experienced, trustworthy guide will walk you through applications (and "Aha!" moments) you never expected from reading the opening chapters of Genesis, showing us how as "Image-Bearers" we are to be more than just faithful stewards but also creative agents.

E. Randolph Richards
Provost and biblical scholar, author of *Misreading Scripture with Western Eyes* and *Rediscovering Jesus*

An essential, expansive, Biblically grounded theology of creativity and a sweeping, deeply researched survey of artisanship and craftsmanship across almost every medium and discipline imaginable. Bil Hood's knowledge and insight into culture is matched if not exceeded by his love for God and deep care for the His creation. For the Christian, an invaluable resource in understanding why His image-bearers are compelled to write, compose, play, and express; and for anyone, no matter where we are in the spiritual life, a light that reveals God's glory, and His own handiwork, in everything we do, whether we know it or not.

Jeff Jensen
Author and Emmy-winning screenwriter; story consultant for Disney and HBO

The Genesis of Creativity is a compelling call to rediscover our divine identity as image-bearers and co-creators, not just in an artistic sense, but through the building of organizational structures and systems. In a world that often stifles innovation, Hood reminds us that true creativity isn't about breaking the mold—it's about reshaping it with purpose and vision. His insights challenge leaders to embrace change, steward their influence, and inspire others to live out their creative calling with boldness and faith. This book is a must-read for anyone leading in today's dynamic ministry landscape.

Jenn Williamson, DMin
Director of Leadership Formation, Missio Nexus

From hovering with intention to releasing with trust, Bil Hood reveals the six divine actions that unlock creativity in every sphere of life. The Genesis of Creativity is not just about making art—it's about discovering how you were designed to create, innovate, and lead with imagination rooted in faith.

Michelle Thompson, PCC, ACTC
Executive Coaching & Consulting

Through my work, I've seen entrepreneurs, artists, and young leaders tap into God-given creativity to build ventures, products, services, and ministries that bless their communities. In *The Genesis of Creativity*, Bil Hood beautifully captures those same principles—creativity flourishing within boundaries, fueled by persistence, faith, and community. This book is a timely and inspiring guide for anyone who longs to imagine, create, and lead with courage.

Baolerhu Ligden
Founder & CEO - *Asia Leadership Network*

The Genesis of Creativity captures what I've seen firsthand in Bil Hood's life and leadership—a humility that listens, a curiosity that seeks, and a faith that creates space for others to shine. This book reminds us that true creativity mirrors God's heart: it builds bridges, not platforms. Bil shows that when our work flows from grace rather than ego, creativity becomes an act of worship and a reflection of the Creator Himself.

Christian Mungai
Global Movement Pastor, *Mariners Church*

Bil Hood's *The Genesis of Creativity* roots our making in the Creator's first work—showing how hovering over chaos, embracing wise boundaries, and creating in community lead to faithful, fruitful art. Pastoral and practical, it frees makers from perfectionism to pursue what is "very good" and then let the work live—this preserves the joyfulness of the creative. These are approaches and strategies that I can personally relate to and vouch for. I gladly commend this book to artists, leaders, and everyday image-bearers.

FLAME (Marcus Gray)
GRAMMY®-nominated hip-hop artist and author

I'm no stranger to the world of art and faith and how these things intersect in life-giving ways. So I was surprised (and delighted!) to discover that Bil Hood's new book, *The Genesis of Creativity*, is filled with ideas that I'd never stopped to ponder—or, as Hood might say, to 'hover over.' Drawing from a trove of contemporary stories, Hood shows us how a creator's process reflects the original 'blueprint' for all creativity: Genesis 1:1–2. This lean and wise work will be manna for all who long to play a part in the new creation.

Heather Choate Davis
Author, Theologian, Songwriter, Minister of Community Engagement

Bil Hood has knocked it out of the park with *The Genesis of Creativity*. This book is fresh, inviting, and profoundly honest—a call to rediscover creativity as both a gift and a responsibility. 'To be human is to be a poem spoken by God. And every act of true creativity—a painting, a friendship, a garden, a gesture of mercy—echoes the beginning.' This book reminds us that creativity is not incidental to faith or life but part of the very fabric of how we relate to the world and to one another."

Tanner Olson
Author and Poet

IN THE BEGINNING, GOD CREATED T
WAS WITHOUT FORM AND VOID, AN
DEEP. AND THE SPIRIT OF GOD WAS
AND GOD SAID, "LET THERE BE LI
SAW THAT THE LIGHT WAS GOOD. A
DARKNESS. GOD CALLED THE LIG
NIGHT. AND THERE WAS EVENING A
AND GOD SAID, "LET THERE BE
WATERS, AND LET IT SEPARATE
GOD MADE THE EXPANSE AND
UNDER THE EXPANSE FROM T
EXPANSE. AND IT WAS SO. AN

...VENS AND THE EARTH. THE EARTH
...KNESS WAS OVER THE FACE OF THE
...NG OVER THE FACE OF THE WATERS.
... AND THERE WAS LIGHT. AND GOD
... SEPARATED THE LIGHT FROM THE
..., AND THE DARKNESS HE CALLED
...ERE WAS MORNING, THE FIRST DAY.
...EXPANSE IN THE MIDST OF THE
...ATERS FROM THE WATERS." AND
...ATED THE WATERS THAT WERE
...ATERS THAT WERE ABOVE THE
...CALLED THE EXPANSE HEAVEN.

the GENESIS of CREATIVITY

What God's First Act Reveals About Your Creative Potential

Bil Hood

© 2026 Hood Creative

All rights reserved. No part of this publication may be reproduced, stored in a retrieval system, or transmitted in any form or by any means—electronic, mechanical, photocopying, recording, or otherwise—without the prior written permission of the publisher.

Scripture quotations are from the Holy Bible, English Standard Version® (ESV), copyright © 2001 by Crossway. Used by permission. All rights reserved. Unless otherwise noted.

Scripture quotations marked (The Message) are from The Message by Eugene H. Peterson, copyright © 1993, 1994, 1995, 1996, 2000, 2001, 2002. Used by permission of NavPress. All rights reserved.

ISBN 979-8-9998580-0-9 (Paperback)

Design by Bil Hood
Printed in the United States of America

Edition 1.2
Library of Congress Control Number: 2025917605

DEDICATION

To the Hoods - past, present, and yet to come,
those who create boldly,
those who wonder if they can be creative,
...and those who have yet to see
the image of the Creator in themselves.

CONTENTS

INTRODUCTION   21
- Chapter One   33
  The Genesis of Creativity

- Chapter Two   47
  The Need for Creativity

THE CREATIVE PROCESS
- Chapter Three   65
  The Genesis of Hovering

- Chapter Four   87
  The Genesis of Identifying

- Chapter Five   111
  The Genesis of Connecting

- Chapter Six   133
  The Genesis of Investing

- Chapter Seven   153
  The Genesis of Persisting

- Chapter Eight   171
  The Genesis of Releasing

WHAT'S NEXT?
- Chapter Nine   189
  Order • Disorder • Reorder

- Chapter Ten   203
  Final Thoughts

LEARN MORE   213
NOTES   229
THANK YOU   247
ABOUT THE AUTHOR   249

NINE DOTS PUZZLE

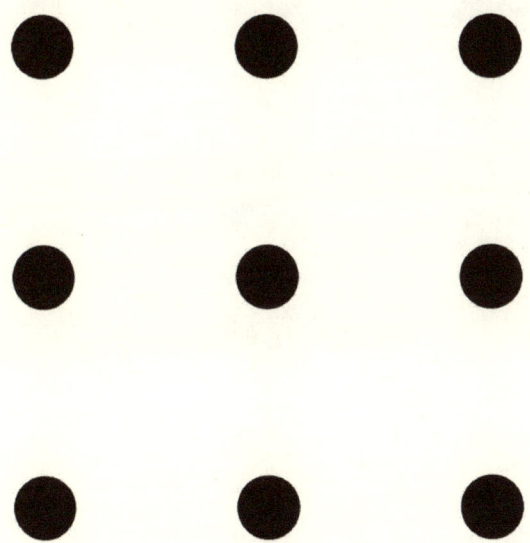

Without lifting your pen,
draw four straight lines that pass through
all nine points above.

the GENESIS of CREATIVITY

The Beginning

In the beginning …

You've heard similar openings before. Fairy tales begin, "Once upon a time." Movies launch with, "A long time ago in a galaxy far, far away." But unlike those stories, this one doesn't begin with fiction; it begins with the reality of creativity. "In the beginning, God created…" The ultimate origin story.

It's a very good place to start.

When I read Genesis 1, I'm not drawn into debates over when it happened, or how, exactly. Those questions intrigue some, but they've never lit a creative fire in me. I'm drawn instead to deeper questions: Who? Why? And, in a broader sense, how?

> *"In the beginning, God created the heavens and the earth. The earth was without form and void, and darkness was over the surface of the deep. And the Spirit of God was hovering over the waters."*
>
> **Genesis 1:1-2**

From the first words, creation is described not as sterile mechanics, but as movement – hovering, identifying, connecting, investing, persisting, and releasing. This is creativity in motion.

Across the days of creation, we'll watch these six divine movements unfold: hovering, identifying, connecting, investing, persisting, and releasing, a rhythm that mirrors every act of human creativity.

Creation begins before the first word spoken. Before creation was an act, it was an idea taking shape in silence. There is always a breath before the beginning, a hovering moment where possibility gathers itself. Every artist, teacher, or parent knows that pause: the heart's quiet inventory before the first brushstroke, the first word, the first decision.

We stand in the same stillness that held the world on the edge of light, feeling both the weight of what might be, and the whisper to begin.

A Creative Inheritance

My family's story taught me that creativity rarely travels in a straight line. It moves like light through stained glass, bending and refracting, coloring everything it touches.

I grew up the grandson of a preacher and the son of an artist, a blend of sermon and sketchpad that shaped how I see the world. My father's design business, Genesis One Design, carried that truth on its door – that all creativity begins with the Creator.

But the seed of this book took root more recently, during my graduate work in leadership through the Townsend Institute. That season helped me see Genesis with new eyes.

Seeing Genesis Anew

Dr. John Townsend, co-author of the well-known book Boundaries, emphasized how intentional limits help people flourish – not just emotionally, but creatively. That insight changed how I read the Creation story. When I returned to Genesis 1 with that lens, I began to see something new.

I saw that God's first creative acts focused on structure.

Light from darkness.

Sky from sea.

Land from water.

It wasn't until these things were in place that God began to fill the world with form and color and movement and life. Not because those early acts were less creative, but because they made creativity possible.

> *It turns out that boundaries don't restrict creativity; they ignite it.*

The more I looked, the more I saw. Not just boundaries, but patterns, rhythms, investments, pauses, risks, relationships. In Genesis 1, God doesn't just create; He models a process. And that process has lessons for anyone who wants to live a more creative life.

What This Book Is, and Isn't

Before we go further, let's clarify what this book is really about. This isn't a book about how old the earth is. It's not a scientific reconstruction of the Big Bang or a theological commentary on cosmology. Instead, it's an invitation to look at Genesis 1 through a different lens – one focused on creativity, intention, and human flourishing.

My hope is that you walk away from these pages with four core realizations.

1) You Were Made in the Image of a Creative God

From the very first verse of Scripture, we're introduced to God not as philosopher, warrior, or judge, but as Creator. Before there are commandments, covenants, or even people, there is creativity. "In the beginning, God created…" That's how the story opens. And that matters.

It tells us something foundational: Creativity is not a hobby for God. It is central to His nature. The first way we come to know God is as the One who brings light from darkness, form from chaos, beauty from the void. The act of creation is the opening note in the symphony of Scripture, and it resonates through every movement that follows.

And then comes the surprise twist:
we are made in that image.

Not merely in the image of a ruler or thinker or moral guide, but in the image of a Creator. Genesis 1:26 tells us that humankind was formed in God's "likeness." That includes the capacity to imagine, to shape, to build, to name, to care, and to bring forth new life and new ideas into the world. Creativity, then, is not optional. It's essential. It's written into our spiritual DNA. To bear the image of God is to participate, however faintly, in the divine rhythm of creation.

You may not think of yourself as an artist. You might not paint, sing, write novels, or design buildings. But if you've ever built a schedule, baked a loaf of bread, solved a problem, launched a business idea, mentored a student, or planted a garden, you've reflected the creativity of your Creator.

Every time you bring order to chaos, light to confusion, or beauty to brokenness, you are mirroring the God who hovered over the waters and said, "Let there be light." Creativity begins there – in the moment you decide that something good can rise from the dark.

2) Creation Is A Pattern Worth Studying

Genesis 1 doesn't just tell us that God created...

It shows us how.

Look at the verbs: God *hovered*, God *separated*, God *saw*, God *blessed*. Each is a movement from chaos to order, from potential to purpose – speech, discernment, distinction, affirmation. They form a rhythm that repeats in every creative act we take: we speak an idea, shape its form, evaluate its goodness, and bless it to live beyond us.

We see God pause and observe before acting. We see Him set boundaries, light from dark, sky from sea, land from water, before filling those spaces with abundance. We see movement and rhythm, call and response, evening and morning. We see evaluation: *"And God saw that it was good."* We even see rest.

These aren't just poetic devices, they are insights into the creative process. They suggest that creativity flourishes not in frenzy, but in rhythm. Not in boundless freedom, but in purposeful boundaries. Not in perfection, but in progression. Each day builds on the last.

Every creative act begins in a kind of darkness. A blank page. A silent room. A problem without a solution. Like God at the beginning, we face a void, formless, uncertain, waiting. But the Spirit still hovers there. Creativity begins when we trust that order, beauty, and purpose can rise from the chaos before us. That's where creation always begins – and begins anew.

These patterns invite us to pay attention to our own creative rhythms.

By studying Genesis 1 not just as a sacred story but as a creative framework, we discover a blueprint that applies to far more than the formation of stars and seas. It applies to how we write, lead, build, parent, teach, invent, heal, dream, and love.

So, as we move through this book, don't just look at the creation story as something that happened once. See it as something still happening, in you, through you, and around you. You are made in the image of a creative God. The creative life isn't for a select few, it's for everyone who bears His image. Which means it's for you.

3) Creativity Is for Everyone

One of the biggest misconceptions about creativity is that it's reserved for a select group – the artists, the musicians, the painters, the poets. Those who work in studios or perform on stages. But creativity is not confined to canvases or concert halls. It is far broader, far deeper, and far more human than that.

Creativity belongs to all of us.

It shows up wherever someone chooses to respond to life with intentionality and imagination, when a teacher reimagines a lesson to reach a struggling student, or a parent turns bedtime into a ritual of wonder and safety. In classrooms and codebases, boardrooms and backyards, creativity flourishes wherever someone asks, "What if something more is possible here?"

You don't have to call yourself an artist to live a creative life. You just have to be willing to see your life as material that can be shaped, stewarded, and offered with purpose.

If you believe in the God of Genesis, I hope this book helps you see that your creativity is not incidental, it's essential. It's part of the divine image you carry. I hope you'll come to know God not just as a creator, but as the Creator, and in turn, discover your own calling to create, restore, imagine, and build in His likeness.

And if you're someone who isn't sure what you believe about God, you're still welcome here. My hope is that you'll find in Genesis 1 more than an origin story, ancient wisdom for a modern creative life. I believe the patterns and insights in these early verses can still speak to our creative life with surprising relevance and clarity.

Because at its core, this book is not about dogma. It's about design. About the rhythm of work and rest, the role of boundaries and risk, and the holy task of bringing something good into a world that needs it.

And in that, I believe, we are all invited.

4) Creativity as Calling

Creativity, at its core, is the sacred act of bringing something new into the world in response to the life you've been given.

It's forming meaning where there was none, shaping order from chaos, infusing beauty into the everyday. That might look like painting a canvas, but it might also look like designing a curriculum, mentoring a teenager, or figuring out dinner from leftovers. Creativity lives wherever intention meets effort.

And that makes creativity more than a skill. It makes it a calling.

In Scripture, callings are rarely glamorous. They are often inconvenient, demanding, and slow to unfold. Think of Moses, stammering through his objections. Or Esther, trembling in the king's court. Or Peter, stepping out onto the water. A true calling always involves risk. It asks for faith. It requires perseverance. And creativity is no different.

To live a creative life is to say yes to uncertainty. To stare down chaos without flinching. To hover before acting. To explore the boundaries instead of escaping them. To make new connections where others see none. To invest yourself, heart and soul, in something that might not work, and might change the world. It means pushing beyond "good enough" toward something that, in God's time and through your faithful effort, may become very good.

And then, perhaps hardest of all, it means letting it go.

Letting it live. Letting your work breathe, adapt, bless, and belong to others. Trusting that the same Spirit who hovered over the deep is still at work in your ideas, your actions, your hopes, and your unfinished drafts.

This is the creative life. It's not just something you do. It's something you step into. It's a calling that echoes the first pages of Scripture and continues through every act of faithful making.

In a world obsessed with speed, novelty, and perfection, creativity reminds us to be patient. To be grounded. To be bold. And to trust that when we reflect the image of the Creator, we are doing holy work.

That's the journey ahead. Chapter by chapter, we'll follow the days of creation: hovering, identifying, connecting, investing, persisting, and releasing. Along the way, we'll meet artists and architects, writers and builders, dreamers and doers. And we'll keep returning to
Genesis 1, not just as sacred text but as a blueprint for creativity in all its forms.

Creativity begins when we join God in bringing order, beauty, and purpose out of chaos.

But why does this calling matter so much today? That's where we turn next.

the GENESIS of CREATIVITY

The Genesis of Creativity

From the first breath of Scripture, we see movement:

God said light, and light broke into being.

God separated light from darkness, sky from sea, land from water.

God saw that it was good, and then He blessed what He made.

These six movements – hovering, identifying, connecting, investing, persisting, and releasing – form the DNA of divine creativity. They trace the pattern of every creative act: attending before acting, discerning boundaries, forming relationships, pouring oneself into the work, staying with it until it is good, and then trusting it to live.

Across Genesis 1, we'll watch these six verbs unfold, a rhythm that mirrors the creative process in every artist, parent, teacher, and leader.

Before anything was formed – before there was time or space or substance, there was communion.

The **Creator** who shapes and blesses. The **Spirit** hovers. The **Word** speaks. God has always existed, not as a solitary being but as a community of love.

This is the first revelation of creativity: it begins in relationship.

Why Create?

The Genesis account doesn't begin with a need, but with a choice. God does not create out of lack but out of desire. A desire to share, to express, to extend the joy of divine fellowship into a world that can respond.

Creation is the outpouring of divine relationship. Each day adds depth to the symphony: light and dark, sea and sky, plants and creatures – each movement distinct yet harmoniously joined. And then, at the crescendo, God creates humanity - not as an afterthought, but as the culmination.

"Let us make mankind in our image, after our likeness ..."

Genesis 1:26

Here, God reveals something breathtaking. Human beings are made in the image of God - *imago Dei*. Not as mere reflections, but as participants. We are not spectators of God's creativity but participants in it. To be human is to be capable of love, meaning, connection, and yes, creativity. We are not divine, but we are designed to echo the divine heart.

And the image of God is not simply about intellect or capacity. It is about communion. We are made to be with God, to walk with each other, to tend the world. From the first chapter of Scripture, human identity is tied to beauty, purpose, and belonging.

In the same way, our best creativity doesn't arise from scarcity or fear but from the overflow of love, curiosity, and connection.

The Imago Dei: Created to Create

Throughout Scripture, we see the echoes of this divine creativity expressed through human hands, sanctified acts, and Spirit-led imagination. The creative impulse placed in humanity at the beginning never fades after Genesis 1;
it reverberates through the stories that follow, testifying to the enduring image of the Creator in us.

When God commissions Bezalel to be the chief artisan of the Tabernacle in *Exodus 31*, He fills him with the Spirit, not for battle or prophecy, but for artistry.

David, the warrior-king, was also a poet and songwriter. His psalms remind us that theology can be sung and lament can be lifted as liturgy.

Jesus, the incarnate Word, taught in parables, drew in the dust, and turned water into wine. His life and ministry reveal not only divine authority, but divine artistry.

Paul, a tentmaker by trade, also built communities with words - his letters are both theology and art. He adapted the gospel to diverse cultures - Athens, Ephesus, Rome - each time using new metaphors, new stories, new language.

Even in Revelation, the final book of Scripture, we find song and architecture, light and color, form and glory. The new creation is not a return to Eden's simplicity, but a fulfillment that incorporates all the artistry of human history into the city of God.

This divine-human creative partnership spans from garden to city, from breath to glory. The image of God is not passive; it calls us to shape the world not just as it is, but as it could be.

We are shown again and again that to be made in the image of God means that creativity is part of our spiritual DNA. We reflect a God who designs, speaks, shapes, and breathes life.

In Genesis, creation begins not from calm but from chaos – formless and void, dark and deep. God's Spirit hovers, not in panic, but in patient possibility. Out of that swirling uncertainty, God brings light, structure, and meaning. We'll return to that moment of hovering in Chapter Three, but for now it reminds us: every creative act begins with attention, not action.

Our own creativity often begins the same way. We stare at the blank page, the empty canvas, the unformed idea. The invitation is not to flee the chaos but to hover over it, to wait, to notice, to discern its boundaries, and to draw forth order, beauty, and purpose from within it.

The Beauty of It All

Genesis does not rush through creation. It lingers. It tells us again and again:

> *"And God saw that it was good."*
>
> **Genesis 1:9**

He didn't rush on to the next task. He paused – to see, to name, to savor the goodness. That pause is part of the creative act itself.

There is wonder here. Not only in the vastness of space or the intricacies of ecosystems, but in the poetic order of the account itself. There is light, there is sky, there is land and life and light again. The world is not thrown together; it is composed.

Science and Scripture together tell the same story of ordered beauty.

Creation sings of God's joy. The color of fruit, the patterns of stars, the rhythms of growth - none of it is accidental.

Beauty is not a side effect. It is a signature.

Science reveals even more: The spiral of a galaxy echoes the spiral of a seashell; the branching of a leaf mirrors our lungs; the rhythm of our heartbeat matches the ocean's tide. In Genesis, beauty isn't decoration - it's declaration. Every color, rhythm, and form says: "This is good."

Scripture also uses beauty as revelation. The psalmist sings, "The heavens declare the glory of God; the skies proclaim the work of His hands" (Psalm 19:1). Jesus said, "Consider the lilies… not even Solomon in all His splendor was dressed like one of these" (Matthew 6:28–29). Creation is theology in visual form.

And in that beauty, we find ourselves, not apart from creation but within it, as caretakers and co–lovers of the world. The artistry of Genesis reminds us that creation is not merely functional; it is relational.

Sustaining Creativity Spiritually

Creativity often begins as a spark of inspiration, but it is sustained by something deeper: discipline, rhythm, and spiritual renewal. The Genesis account offers not only a vision of beginnings but a guide to endurance.

The first chapter of Genesis shows us inspiration; the second teaches us integration, how creativity becomes a way of life.

If Genesis 1 shows us how creation begins, Genesis 2 shows us how it endures. Creativity isn't only inspiration – it's rhythm: work, rest, renewal.

The Role of Rest

After six days of creation, God rests. This rest is not due to exhaustion but to fulfillment. It is the Creator's declaration that the work is good and complete.

> *"By the seventh day God had finished the work he had been doing; so on the seventh day he rested from all his work. Then God blessed the seventh day and made it holy."*
>
> **Genesis 2:2-3**

Rest is not a retreat from creativity – it is part of the creative process. In resting, we recognize that our work is not our identity. We are invited into a rhythm that includes reflection, gratitude, and renewal.

This rhythm becomes especially important in a culture driven by output. Our worth, we are told, is found in what we produce.

But God declares something else: the work is done, and it is good. And rest affirms that.

Sabbath is also an act of resistance.

In *Exodus 20*, the Sabbath commandment is tied to creation. In *Deuteronomy 5*, it is tied to liberation: "Remember that you were slaves in Egypt and that the Lord your God brought you out…"

Rest is both recognition of creation and rejection of slavery. It is a spiritual act that says: I am not a machine. I am a beloved creation.

God's rest wasn't withdrawal but delight. He didn't step away from His creation - He stepped into it.

Prayer and Meditation

Creativity requires space not just in our schedules, but in our souls. Prayer opens that space. It invites God into our questions, frustrations, and longings. It reminds us that we are not creating alone.

Meditation – dwelling in Scripture, sitting in silence, listening to God's Spirit – can rekindle insight and courage. It centers us not on our productivity, but on our connection to the One who made us.

"Be still and know that I am God."

Psalm 46:10

Stillness is not passivity; it is receptivity. In that quiet, new vision can emerge. It is in the space between striving that the seeds of creativity grow.

Many creatives throughout history practiced this rhythm. Johann Sebastian Bach signed his compositions '*Soli Deo Gloria*', To God alone be the glory, because for him, creativity was worship. Flannery O'Connor prayed not only for inspiration but for the discipline to follow through. Dorothy Day's activism flowed from a deeply meditative spirituality. Even Brother Lawrence found meaning in washing dishes when done in the presence of God.

Just as the Spirit hovered before creation, so prayer teaches us to hover – to wait, to listen, to attend.

The Sabbath as a Creative Reset

The Sabbath is more than a day off. It is a sacred interruption, a pause that resets our perspective and restores our imagination. A recalibration of the heart.
By practicing Sabbath, we step into a pattern of trust – trust that God holds all things, including our work.

It is easy for creative people to believe the lie that we must always be producing. But the Sabbath reminds us: our value is not in what we make, but in who we are. We are beloved. And in that belovedness, our creativity finds space to breathe.

This reset also fosters imagination. When we stop, we begin to see. When we rest, we begin to listen. When we delight, we begin to dream again.

The Sabbath isn't the end of work - it's what makes work creative again.

A Creative Legacy

Genesis 1 is not merely a theological preface. Rather, it is a declaration: we were made by a relational Creator, in love, for love. Our creativity is not about productivity or fame; it is about communion. It flows from our design.
It reflects our origin.

To be human is to be a poem spoken by God. And every act of true creativity – a painting, a friendship,
a garden, a gesture of mercy – echoes the beginning. These acts are not incidental to faith; they are part of the fabric of how we relate to the world and to one another.

Our legacy as image–bearers is one of beauty-making, justice-seeking, and culture–forming. We are called to take the raw materials of our world – our time, our words, our communities, our griefs and joys – and make something that reflects God's goodness. This calling isn't always easy. Sometimes we create in the midst of brokenness. Sometimes we create in defiance of despair. But always, we create with hope.

And that raises the question at the heart of the next chapter: If we were made to create, then why do we need creativity today more than ever?

Why does this ancient calling matter in a digital, distracted, divided world? What does creativity look like in the face of chaos, injustice, or exhaustion? What might it look like for us to reclaim our role as co-creators with God - not just in theory, but in the world we actually inhabit?

Creativity is not a relic of Eden – it's the rhythm of restoration. The God who made light from darkness still calls us to bring beauty from chaos.

Pause and Reflect

Creativity is more than an origin story - it is a present calling. Before you turn the page, take a moment to consider how you reflect the image of a Creator in your daily life.

Questions to Consider:

In what ways do I express creativity,
even if I don't think of myself as an artist?

How does seeing God as Creator
change how I see myself?

Where do I feel the tension between creativity
and constraint in my life right now?

"God is really another artist.
He invented the giraffe,
the elephant and the cat.
He has no real style.
He just goes on trying other things."

Pablo Picasso

46

the NEED FOR CREATIVITY

"Everybody born comes from
the Creator trailing wisps of glory.
We come from the Creator with creativity.
I think that each one of us is born with creativity."

Maya Angelou

"There is no doubt that creativity is
the most important human resource of all.
Without creativity, there would be no progress,
and we would be forever
repeating the same patterns."

Edward de Bono

The Need For Creativity

We live in a time defined by rapid technological advancements, where creativity reigns as a prized skill. Yet, despite its acknowledged importance, creativity remains elusive and challenging to define. It often begins in chaos, a void full of ideas, and emerges as solutions, innovations, and breakthroughs. The process of moving from chaos to creation is where creativity flourishes. But what happens during this transformative process? And how can we better navigate this space to harness our own creative potential?

Creativity isn't just for artists or inventors. It's taught, measured, and monetized across industries, leadership off-sites, design studios, classrooms, kitchens, garages. The emphasis is clear: creativity fuels progress.

Despite this widespread focus, the pursuit of creativity is anything but new. In *Genesis* chapter 4, we meet the descendants of Cain. People living outside Eden yet still bearing the creative image of God. Seven generations after Cain come Jabal, Jubal, and Tubal-Cain, the founders of animal husbandry, instrumental music, and metalwork. These aren't prophets or priests; they're builders, artisans, and musicians. The Bible's first depiction of cultural innovation doesn't come from a throne or a temple, but from ordinary people shaping tools, sounds, and systems. Even in exile, humanity's creative drive carries forward God's imprint. Creativity, from the very beginning, is portrayed not as a luxury but a calling woven into the human experience.

Even east of Eden, you can trace the same pattern: identifying problems, connecting materials and people, investing effort and skill, persisting through risk, and releasing gifts that serve the community.

The Science of Creativity

Modern science and technology have illuminated the mechanics of creativity. We now understand it as the act of turning imaginative ideas into reality. It involves perceiving the world uniquely, finding patterns, and making connections between seemingly unrelated ideas. This ability has propelled humanity through eras of profound transformation, from the agricultural age to the industrial age, the information age, and now, the emerging conceptual age.

Neuroscience has revealed that creativity is a whole-brain activity, engaging both the analytical left hemisphere and the intuitive right hemisphere. Functional MRI scans show that creative thinking activates regions associated with memory, emotion, and problem-solving. This interplay of networks enables us to hover with attention, identify patterns, connect distant ideas, invest effort, persist through iteration, and finally release solutions.

A recent Adobe study on creativity revealed that eight in ten people view it as crucial to economic development, while nearly two-thirds believe it is valuable to society. Creativity is increasingly recognized as a vital skill for the modern workplace. Yet the same study found that many individuals feel they fall short of their creative potential.

Why?

Misconceptions About Creativity

Part of the challenge lies in our narrow definition of creativity. When asked to name creative figures, people often point to historical icons like Michelangelo or Mozart. This focus on groundbreaking masterpieces represents "Big–C" creativity, exceptional works that leave a lasting cultural impact. But most creativity in daily life is more subtle. Referred to as "little–c" creativity, it includes problem–solving at work, improvements in household routines, or innovative approaches to school projects.

Dan Pallotta, writing in *Harvard Business Review*, observes, "The best creativity comes from a desire to contribute to the lives of others, either by introducing something new that improves their quality of life or by showing them that something thought to be impossible is, in fact, possible." Creativity, then, is not just about artistic expression but also about fostering hope and changing perceptions. Big or small, the same six movements apply.

Creativity in the Workplace

In 2010, IBM conducted a global CEO study that surveyed over 1,500 CEOs across 60 countries and 33 industries. The study revealed that creativity was the most essential leadership quality, ranking higher than integrity, global thinking, and even vision. Yet, despite its importance, creativity in the workplace often falters under the weight of risk aversion. Creative solutions require the freedom to experiment, and fail. Organizations that foster a culture of psychological safety, where employees feel supported in taking creative risks, are more likely to see innovation flourish.

Research from the Yale Center for Emotional Intelligence highlights this dynamic: people are more willing to share original ideas when they know there will be no negative social consequences. Companies that prioritize creativity see tangible benefits; they are 3.5 times more likely to outperform their peers in revenue growth.

Creativity in the workplace often involves challenging traditional ways of thinking. For instance, design–thinking methodologies encourage employees to empathize with users, define problems clearly, brainstorm freely, and prototype iteratively. This process not only fosters innovation but also empowers teams to take ownership of their creative contributions. Empathy maps and prototypes formalize hovering and identifying before teams invest, persist, and release.

Leaders play a crucial role in setting the conditions for creativity to flourish. Effective leaders model creative behavior by demonstrating curiosity, taking calculated risks, and showing a willingness to embrace failure as part of the process. They also invest in creating environments where creativity can thrive, spaces that promote collaboration, provide access to diverse perspectives, and offer the time and resources necessary for experimentation.

One of the biggest barriers to workplace creativity is the fear of failure. Organizations that succeed in fostering innovation often adopt practices that destigmatize failure. Celebrating lessons learned from unsuccessful attempts rather than punishing them, encourages employees to think boldly and pursue ambitious ideas. For many years, Google's "20% Time" policy, which allowed employees to dedicate a portion of their time to passion projects, has resulted in some of the company's most successful products, including Gmail and Google Maps. The policy was designed to allow employees to spend up to 20% of their work time on projects that interested them, even if those projects were not part of their official job responsibilities. This policy encouraged innovation, creativity, and experimentation, including the possibility of failure.

The policy created an environment where employees could take risks, explore new ideas, and learn from failures without fear of immediate repercussions.

Different viewpoints and an open culture are also key drivers of creativity in the workplace. Teams composed of individuals with varied backgrounds, experiences, and perspectives are better equipped to approach problems from multiple angles. This diversity enhances the team's ability to generate novel ideas and innovate effectively. Research from McKinsey & Company shows that companies with higher levels of gender and ethnic diversity are significantly more likely to outperform their peers in profitability and innovation.

The physical work environment can also influence creativity. Open, flexible spaces that encourage movement and collaboration can spark spontaneous discussions and idea sharing. However, it's equally important to provide quiet areas where employees can focus and reflect. Balancing these needs ensures that individuals with different working styles can contribute their best creative efforts.

Finally, technology is transforming the creative landscape in workplaces. Tools powered by Artificial Intelligence (AI) are enabling teams to analyze data, identify patterns, and automate repetitive tasks, freeing up time for more complex and imaginative work. Collaboration platforms like Slack and Miro facilitate communication and idea sharing across distributed teams, breaking down barriers that once limited creativity.

By cultivating a workplace culture that values creativity, organizations can unlock untapped potential, drive innovation, and position themselves for long-term success in an ever-changing world.

Creativity in Education

Despite its importance, creativity in schools is declining. Dr. Kyung Hee Kim, an educational psychologist, has studied creativity scores among U.S. students and found a significant decrease since 1990, particularly in younger grades. One contributing factor is the emphasis on standardized testing since the *No Child Left Behind Act* of 2001. While the intent was to ensure academic success, the result has been a sidelining of arts and music programs, key avenues for fostering creativity. We've taught outcomes while neglecting hovering and identifying; we test answers more than we teach connecting and persisting.

The issue is compounded by an educational system that prioritizes rote memorization and test performance over critical thinking and creative exploration. Students are often rewarded for providing the "right" answers rather than generating novel ideas or challenging assumptions. This creates a learning environment that values conformity over originality.

In contrast, countries like Hungary, Japan, and the Netherlands balance high academic performance with robust arts education. These nations recognize that creativity is not just an extracurricular activity but a core component of a well-rounded education. Their curricula integrate arts, music, and hands-on projects alongside traditional subjects, fostering a holistic approach to learning.

The Adobe *Creativity and Education* study underscores the importance of creativity in learning environments. While

57 percent of college students see creativity as very important, the number rises dramatically to 78 percent among those who believe creativity is essential for their careers. Yet, 82 percent of respondents wish they had more exposure to creative thinking during their school years. This disconnect highlights a need for systemic change.

Schools that emphasize creativity often adopt interdisciplinary approaches to teaching. For example, project-based learning encourages students to tackle real-world problems by combining knowledge from multiple subjects. A science class might collaborate with an art class to design and build sustainable models of urban environments, blending technical skills with aesthetic considerations.

At Concordia University Irvine this is expressed through their Enduring Questions & Ideas (Q&I) Core curricula. The most unique feature of the Q&I Core is its pairing of classes that at first glance don't seem to go together, biology and theology, mathematics and philosophy, history and literature. "Concordia's Q&I program helps students grow into critical and meaningful thinkers. Through the lens of disciplines such as biology, English, and philosophy, professors encourage students to discuss some of life's biggest questions like the nature of goodness, truth, and beauty," says Makenna Myers, a double major in English and in Humanities & Fine Arts. Those pairings force students to hover with big questions, identify assumptions, and connect disciplines before they invest in arguments and release their work.

Technology also offers opportunities to enhance creativity in education. Digital tools like coding platforms, virtual reality experiences, and video editing software enable students to express their ideas in innovative ways. Additionally, online collaboration platforms facilitate group projects, allowing students to share and refine their work with peers across the globe.

Teachers play a pivotal role in fostering creativity. Educators who encourage open–ended questions, celebrate diverse perspectives, and provide constructive feedback create an environment where students feel empowered to take creative risks. Professional development programs can equip teachers with the tools and strategies needed to nurture creativity in their classrooms.

Parental involvement is another key factor. Parents who expose their children to diverse experiences, such as visits to museums, participation in community theater, or exploration of nature, lay the foundation for creative thinking. Encouraging curiosity at home helps children develop the confidence to explore new ideas and challenge conventional thinking.

To reverse the decline in creativity scores, schools must embrace a cultural shift that prioritizes innovation alongside academic achievement. By integrating arts and creative thinking into the core curriculum, educators can prepare students not only to succeed in standardized tests but also to thrive in a rapidly changing world.

Creativity at Home

The home is one of the most important spaces for nurturing creativity. It is often within the safety and familiarity of our homes that our first imaginative sparks are kindled. From childhood play to adult hobbies, the home provides a fertile ground for exploration and experimentation.

Homes are laboratories for hovering (unstructured time), identifying (naming constraints), and connecting (people, materials, ideas).

Parents play a pivotal role in fostering creativity at home. Simple activities, such as storytelling, drawing, or building with blocks, can ignite a child's imagination and encourage problem-solving skills. Setting aside time for unstructured play allows children to explore their ideas without fear of judgment or failure. Providing access to diverse materials, art supplies, books, or even household items, can inspire creativity in unexpected ways.

For adults, creativity at home often emerges through hobbies and personal projects. Gardening, cooking, crafting, or writing are all ways to exercise creative muscles. These activities not only bring joy but also help relieve stress and provide a sense of accomplishment. Collaborative projects, such as designing a family photo album or redecorating a room, can strengthen relationships while sparking innovation.

Technology has expanded the possibilities for home-based creativity. Online platforms like YouTube, Pinterest, and Skillshare offer endless tutorials and inspiration for creative pursuits. Virtual workshops and communities connect individuals with shared interests, allowing them to learn from and collaborate with others around the world.

Creating a home environment that supports creativity involves more than providing tools and resources. It requires cultivating an atmosphere of curiosity and openness. Asking questions like "What if?" or "How might we?" can prompt innovative thinking. Encouraging family members to share their ideas and celebrating their efforts, regardless of the outcome, reinforces the value of creative exploration.

One powerful way to foster creativity at home is by embracing challenges as opportunities. When faced with a problem, whether it's organizing a cluttered space or planning a family event, approaching it with a creative mindset can lead to unexpected and satisfying solutions. Involving all members of the household in brainstorming and problem-solving can also build a collaborative spirit and generate fresh perspectives.

Finally, downtime and reflection are essential for creativity. Quiet moments allow the mind to wander and make new connections. Whether it's taking a walk, journaling, quiet commutes, or simply daydreaming, these periods of rest can lead to breakthroughs and inspire new ideas. Stillness is not absence; it's hovering.

By nurturing creativity at home, families can create a foundation for innovation that extends into every aspect of life. The home becomes not just a place of comfort but a wellspring of inspiration and ingenuity. Our creativity at home also impacts our health and well-being.

Creativity and Health

The relationship between creativity and well-being is another area of growing interest. Studies have shown that engaging in creative activities reduces stress, improves mental health, and fosters a sense of purpose. Expressive writing, for instance, has been linked to improved immune function, while activities like painting and music therapy have been shown to alleviate symptoms of anxiety and depression.

Creativity also enhances cognitive function. Activities that require problem-solving or learning new skills stimulate neural pathways, keeping the brain active and healthy. This is particularly important as people age, since creative pursuits can help delay cognitive decline and improve overall quality of life.

Moreover, the therapeutic benefits of creativity extend to physical health. Participating in artistic activities has been shown to lower blood pressure, reduce cortisol levels, and promote relaxation. Creative expression allows individuals to process emotions and cope with stress more effectively, contributing to a healthier and more balanced life.

Communities that embrace artistic expression and innovation often see enhanced social cohesion and economic vitality. Public art projects, for example, not only beautify neighborhoods but also inspire civic pride and collaboration. Shared creative experiences, such as community theater or group art classes, foster connections among participants and create a sense of belonging.

Workplaces and schools are increasingly recognizing the link between creativity and health. Companies are introducing wellness programs that incorporate creative activities, such as painting workshops or mindfulness exercises, to improve employee morale and productivity. Similarly, schools that integrate arts and creative play into their curricula often report improved student well-being and engagement.

Ultimately, the healing power of creativity lies in its ability to connect us to ourselves and to others. Whether through individual pursuits or collaborative efforts, creativity offers a pathway to greater resilience, fulfillment, and joy.

A Legacy of Creativity

Interestingly, some of humanity's greatest inventions, the printing press, the light bulb, the airplane, predate modern digital technologies. A recent National Geographic list of "10 Inventions That Changed the World" highlights innovations such as the wheel and the clock, which continue to shape our lives today. More recent advancements, including the iPhone and blockchain technology, build upon these foundational ideas.

This progression underscores an essential truth: creativity is not a finite resource. Instead, it is a renewable force, continuously evolving and adapting to meet the needs of each generation. By embracing both the chaos and the constraints of the creative process, we can unlock possibilities that shape a brighter future.

Creativity is not just a tool for solving problems or advancing careers, it is a vital force that enriches every aspect of life. It begins in the same place Genesis does, not in a blank canvas, but in a world of swirling chaos and potential. Like God, we create best when we bring rhythm, intention, and purpose, hovering, identifying, connecting, investing, persisting, and releasing.

Creativity doesn't always begin with action. Sometimes, it begins with presence. In the following chapter, we'll return to the beginning. Not just to read the creation story, but to study its form, its flow, and the divine blueprint it offers for a life of creativity. Before a single word was spoken, the Spirit hovered; we will practice that first movement, learning to hold space, pay attention, and prepare for what God will help us release.

Pause and Reflect

The world pushes us to act fast, to produce more, to fix what is broken. But what if the first step isn't doing, it's hovering? What if creativity begins in the silence, when we are most attentive, most present?

Questions to Consider:

In what areas of your life are you feeling a pull toward creativity?

How might pausing before acting lead to deeper insight or clarity?

Where do you need to hover before moving forward?

What does stillness look like in your current season of life?

"Think left and think right, think low and think high. Oh, the things you can think if only you try!"

Dr. Seuss

"Information is not knowledge.
The only source of knowledge is experience."

Albert Einstein

"I have no special talent.
I am only passionately curious."

Albert Einstein

Hover Above the Chaos

First this: God created the Heavens and Earth—all you see, all you don't see. Earth was a soup of nothingness, a bottomless emptiness, an inky blackness. God's Spirit brooded like a bird above the watery abyss."

Genesis 1:1-2 - THE MESSAGE

In the beginning, God created the heavens and the earth. 2 The earth was without form and void, and darkness was over the face of the deep. And the Spirit of God was hovering over the face of the waters.

Genesis 1:1-2 ESV

This is the beginning.

The following is the description of the very beginning of the very beginning:

Some translations say that the Spirit of God brooded over the waters.

That single word opens a window. Translated as *brooded* or *hovered*, it comes from the Hebrew verb *rachaph* (רָחַף). It's a rare word, used only a few times in the entire Hebrew Bible. One of its clearest parallels comes from *Deuteronomy 32:11*, in the poetic Song of Moses:

> *"Like an eagle that stirs up its nest, that flutters (rachaph) over its young, spreading out its wings, catching them, bearing them on its pinions."*
>
> **Deuteronomy 32:11**

Here, rachaph describes a mother eagle hovering protectively, attentively, even tenderly, over her young, ready to shelter, nurture, or catch them when they fall. This is not a detached act. It's relational. Responsive. Intimate.

So, when we read in *Genesis 1:2* that the Spirit of God was hovering over the face of the waters, it's not a passive image. It's a pregnant pause, a poised stillness, full of attentive care and readiness to act. God is not only observing the chaos but hovering with intention, waiting for just the right moment to speak order into being.

This divine hovering suggests that the creative process does not begin with doing, it begins with presence. With attention. With hovering.

Before God says, "Let there be light," God is there, hovering. Preparing. Protecting. Imagining. And that hovering becomes a sacred act of creative readiness.

In the beginning, there was the chaos of the waters. God took time to hover.

Here we see God, hovering or brooding, putting in the effort to fully catalog and curate the situation. It leaves a sense of timelessness. That God hovered for ages. Marinated in the chaos, observing, identifying, protecting, and maybe even urgently planning for a change for the good. This seems to be confirmed by the very next step: 'Let there be light.' Light drives out the darkness. Light exposes the reality. Light brings into focus all that lies before.

The Beatles

Probably one of the least offensive statements you can make these days, is "I love The Beatles!" It is right up there with "I love ice cream" or "I love getting a good night's sleep". That said, I do love The Beatles. I was born two weeks after the *White Album* was released. *Hey Jude* had just finished a nine-week run at number one. The music of The Beatles is some of the first music that I can remember my mom playing around the house. Through the years, their music has been more than a soundtrack to my life, at times it was the goal I was chasing.

When I was in high school, my best friend, David, got to start taking guitar lessons. Paying for private lessons was not in the cards for me. So, on Saturdays, I would go over to Dave's house and have him show me everything he learned at the previous weeks lesson. Armed with that new knowledge, I would go home to my guitar and my Big Book of Beatles Music. It had simplified guitar chords for many of the biggest hits. The music of The Beatles was the music I learned guitar to.

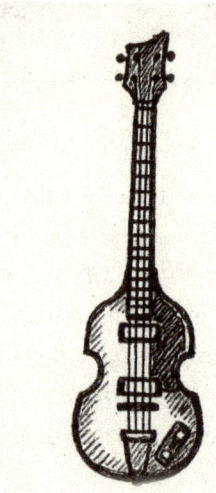

Later in college, I happened upon a bass guitar in a secondhand store in Montana's Flathead Valley. It was a cheap, knock-off of Paul McCartney's Hofner bass. I spent the better part of a week returning to the store to try and get them to bring the price down to the $50 cash I had in my pocket. It was a great win for me to drive the bass home to Seattle. Years later, the bass was joined in my guitar collection by a Rickenbacker 350 Fireglo guitar. It was the spitting image of the guitar George Harrison played. This is the guitar that supplied the unique sounds on songs like: *A Hard Day's Night, Can't Buy Me Love*, and *Ticket to Ride*. In addition to finding gear that let me look like a Beatle, I also have logged the lyrics to their songs deep in my memory. I would guess that I could sing along to every Beatles song and get the lyrics 99% correct. And I am giving the 1 percent because the task would take more than 20 hours covering 440 songs (according to the Complete Beatles playlist on Spotify).

All of this led to a big day for me in the early '90s. I was working in downtown Seattle at a firm that produced major corporate events and communications. Our offices were across the hall from Sub Pop records and across the street from the Moore Theater. An area of town that was ground zero for the rise of grunge. But, what caught my ear that day was the news that Paul and Linda McCartney would be appearing just four blocks away at the Seattle Art Museum. They were in town to hock their new vegetarian microwave meals, or something like that. As soon as I had a break in my work, I tore a page out of The Beatles calendar that was hanging above my desk, grabbed a Sharpie, and hustled up Second Avenue to see what might happen.

I have always lived life with the attitude that – if you act like you belong, you can get yourself into a lot of places. Armed with that attitude, I decided to head through a door that took me to the loading dock under the museum. My thoughts were that, anywhere else in the building, I would probably be stopped by ropes or security. I wasn't long wandering the halls when a door opened across from me a big, bodyguard-looking guy walked through followed by Sir Paul McCartney. He was so gracious. In my mind, I looked like a starstruck fan and hopefully not a creepy stalker. He approached me, shook my hand, asked my name, and asked if the Sharpie was for him to use. I still have the autograph hanging in my office today.

My love of The Beatles has led me to watch a lot of movies and documentaries, and read plenty of books, about them. Something that has always struck me about The Beatles was the way they used their first several years as a band.

Before The Beatles became the global phenomenon of we know, they hovered.

First, they needed to observe the limitations that they were handed. Ultimately a 4-piece band, they were limited to the notes in a musical scale, the number of minutes of music that could fit on a record, the sounds that were available from each of their instruments, and to search for things they may have missed.

They spent a lot of time brooding and hovering.

The Beatles first started coming together in 1957. They were just school kids. During the early years, they played where they could for a few years. First as the part of the Quarrymen, then Johnny and the Moondogs, then the Silver Beetles, before settling on The Beatles. In early 1960, their unofficial manager, Allan Williams arranged for them to play a residency in Hamburg. This was something they did a couple of times. It was a way to immerse the band into music. When in Hamburg, they ate, drank, and slept music. They were paid £2.50 each a day, seven days a week, playing nearly all day. Lennon said: "We had to play for hours and hours on end. Every song lasted twenty minutes and had twenty solos in it. That's what improved the playing."

As a group, they learned to manage, or curate, their music in Germany. Playing 5-6 shows a day for months, hundreds of shows in a row without a break. Living their music from the time they woke up until the time they went to sleep. Honing and perfecting. Learning about how people react to different songs in different ways. This time in Germany coalesced them as a team and forged their talent in a way that only time and repetition can.

I like to think of this as The Beatles "hovering" period. They would play every night, often from 7pm until 3am. They marinated themselves in music. Being a relatively new group, they drew from the artists they loved, often playing cover songs. This was an incubator that allowed the group to explore all the nooks and crannies of music.

When you step back and try to look at music logically, it seems to have some tight boundaries. An octave in traditional western music only has 7 whole notes - A, B, C, D, E, F, G – supported by 5 flats or sharps distributed between them. There are a limited number of ways to sequence these notes, or even the chords that they can combine to make. Add to that limited number of octaves of their chosen instruments. Then with The Beatles, they were limited by the number of players and voices they could combine to get their sounds. But their hovering period set them up for what became an unprecedented run in music.

If they were in the club in Hamburg for almost fifty hours a week, over their first run of forty-eight days, they logged nearly 2,500 hours of music in that first residency. Those dates were followed by a ninety-two-date run in '61. Add to that rehearsal time, song writing time, and the other dates they played, they easily hit 10,000 hours as a band by the end of 1961, hovering over music. 10,000 hours is the magic number that Malcolm Gladwell identifies as the time needed to become a world-class expert in a skill. This gave The Beatles an intense time to get to know all aspects of their craft.

Coming out of Hamburg The Beatles were poised to make a big musical statement. In 1963 they released their first album, *Please Please Me*, and never looked back. *Billboard* lists The Beatles as the artist with the most number 1 hits (20). Songs with the most weeks at number 1 (3 at 12 weeks). Most number one hits in a year (6). Most number one albums in the U.S. all time (19). Most albums in the Billboard top 200 albums of all time

(5). In the U.K. The Beatles spent more time at number one (176 weeks) than any other artist. They also have the most number one albums of all time (15).

So much of this success traces back to those early years.

Their time in Hamburg wasn't just about time spent performing; it was a season of creative incubation. They didn't yet have a distinct sound, but they had time. They studied audience reactions, tested arrangements, copied their heroes, and found their own voice within constraints. Like God hovering over chaotic waters, they marinated in the noise until something new began to take form.

The years spent hovering around the music scene.

Observing
Curating
Marinating

To see the light, we first need to observe, curate, and marinate in our chaos.

Observe

In my experience, hovering over a problem helps you understand all of the opportunities available to help move toward a creative solution.

Taking time to explore all the factors that could impact the next move.

Identifying all the tools at your disposal.

Looking into ways that others may have approached similar situations.

This understanding and perceiving can be a key to our own grasp of the boundaries that we work within and the framework that may contain the solution. It all reminds me of the book *Flatland* by Edwin Abbott.

Flatland is a satire describing a two-dimensional world organized by a strict caste system of geometrical forms. The narrator, A. Square, introduces us to the features of Flatland before recounting his explorations of Lineland, a one-dimensional world, and Pointland, a world of no dimensions, and then the inconceivable three-dimensional world of Spaceland. Everyone that the Square encounters can't understand the dimensions that have been discovered.

The inhabitants of Pointland have never shifted their perspective to see that what appears to be a point, may be the beginning of a line. In Lineland, women are thin, straight lines (the lowliest of shapes), and men have any number of sides depending on their social status. Square ends up in Spaceland, a three-dimensional world that he had never been able to conceive before.

It is a reminder that we may at times allow ourselves to be confined by the way things have always been. That we need to find ways to brood and hover over our situation to make sure that we have all the facts and options in hand.

Don't dismiss anything at this point. You may find that what appears to be random will fit together later. Find ways to let go of what you thought the solution might be and allow yourself to be carried where life takes you. As you hover, and brood, and observe, and research you may find that you become all eyes, seeing things in new ways.

Another way to think about it is the difference between observing and simply seeing. Observing is something deeper. My family has been fans of the TV show *Psych* since the beginning. We watched it as they originally aired and have gone back and binged all the episodes a couple of times. In the show Shawn Spencer plays the lead character. He claims to have special psychic powers that help the local police solve cases. But he really only has a higher level of observation than those around him. It is a similar plot line to the TV show *The Mentalist* (another family favorite) and the storied career of Sherlock Holmes.

Hovering in action

Mavuno Church in Nairobi dared to dream big. They wanted to set an audacious goal, a vision for what their small local church could become. Their mission was already clear: transforming their members into Fearless Leaders. But they wanted more. Could God have plans for them that they hadn't yet pursued?

To seek this next step, the leaders of the church retreated to the tallest building in Nairobi. From that unique vantage point, they hovered over the city, praying, pacing, and planning. As they observed the vastness of Nairobi and its neighborhoods, their vision expanded. They no longer saw just their city, but an opportunity to impact all of Africa and beyond.

From that moment came a bold plan: to plant churches in key neighborhoods of Nairobi, every capital city in Africa, and the gateway cities of the world. What started as a time of observation and prayer transformed into a clear, God-sized mission.

Since 2005, Mavuno Church has turned this vision into reality. They have planted five churches in Nairobi, expanded into four other African nations, and even established a church in Berlin, Germany - a gateway city to Europe.

What began with hovering above the chaos led to purposeful action, proving that time spent in prayerful observation can uncover opportunities far beyond imagination.

Like the Spirit hovering over the waters, their time of prayerful observation became the seed of divine imagination.

In *A Scandal in Bohemia*, Sherlock Holmes explains the difference between seeing and observing to Watson:

"When I hear you explain your reasoning," Watson commented, "the question always seems so ridiculously simple to me, that I feel sure that I could easily have made the same deductions as you. However, to each new case that appears to me of its apparently strange powers, I feel confused until you explain the process that followed and nevertheless, I think I have as good eyes as you."

"It's possible," he said dropping into an armchair. "You see, but don't observe. The distinction is perfectly clear. For example, you have often seen the staircase leading from the lobby to this room."

"Certainly."

"How often?"

"Well, several hundred times"

"Then, you can tell me how many steps there are."

"How many steps? I don't know."

"Do you understand now? You haven't observed, despite having seen. That's what I wanted to tell you. Now, I know that there are seventeen steps because I have seen and observed."

There is research that points to the need for observation as a catalyst to creativity. Researchers at the University of Amsterdam have studied the relationship between observation, mindfulness and creativity. The results of those studies show that strong observation skills are linked to greater creativity, originality, and flexible thinking.

So, how do we develop our powers of observation? A blog post by Kevin Eikenberry has been one of the better guides I have seen. In the post he identifies six steps to become more observant.

Be Open

This speaks to the *Flatland* of it all. Be ready to observe things you didn't expect. Be ready for inspiration to come from places you don't expect. Be willing to accept what you observe.

Be Intentional

The Beatles were intentional. They sought out new music that they appreciated. They took the time to learn the songs of their heroes. This does speak to a need for focus. Know what your goals are and line up your observations next to those goals. Be intentional about your observations.

Be Looking

Once you are open and intentional, be looking. Keep your goal top of mind as you encounter new observations. But don't think it only means looking.

Be Multi-Sensory

Use more than your eyes. Eikenberry says that "True observation is multi-sensory". Allow input from all your senses. Also understand that there is a heart component to observing. I also take this to mean multi-sourced. Talk to others. Watch/read/listen to all kinds of content, both non-fiction and fiction. You never know what might connect

Be Still

It is hard to be observant when your nose is in your phone. It is hard to be observant when you are constantly talking. It is hard to be observant when you are the center of attention, and always on the move. Without stillness you may miss a lot of what you need to launch creativity.

Be Aware of Your Filters

Often when observing we allow past experiences and habits, or our personal beliefs to act as a gatekeeper that will keep observations out. It really loops back to the first point, Be Open.

In short Creativity begins with observation. Yogi Berra said, "You can see lot just by observing." Often everything I need is there to be seen. What we need to do is begin to collect all the observable data. After hovering over an opportunity, collecting the observations we move to the next key starting phase, curating.

Curate

Now that you have collected your observations it's time to curate them. Find ways to connect things that may have not been connected. Identify the great ideas among the distractions. Separate the wheat from the chaff.

To curate is to sift and select. It is the sacred work of making meaning from abundance, deciding what to keep, what to combine, and what to leave behind.

I have used many ways to curate. It really depends on the goal, the task, and the number of observations collected. Often the simpler the project the easier it is to do this in my own head. I have never been mind-palace guy, but it worked for ancient Rome and Greece, and still works for people today. The ancients called it Loci – it was a way to commit large amounts of information to memory by tying them to specific visual and spatial memories or locations. *Moonwalking with Einstein* by Joshua Foer is a great book about improving memory.

Music has always been a great way for me to memorize details. Growing up, my mom would always help my brother and me with our school memorization by making up songs for our spelling words or memory verses.

The best way for me to curate large amounts of information is visually. Sometimes I like to use digital tools like Miro or Evernote. These allow for simple linking to content outside my own thoughts and are great for inviting others into a group-think situation. I also find that the older I get the more I need to text myself observations or create a note on my phone that I add to as new information arises.

Sometimes I can look like your typical TV conspiracy nutjob when my curation ends up on note cards and Post-its tacked to my wall with strings showing the connections. That's the way this book started to take shape.

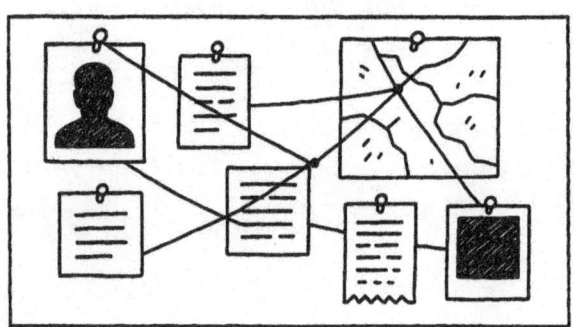

Marinate

Now that we have observed and curated, it is time to marinate.

I know that marinate is a cooking term, but it stuck with me ever since I heard it used in a sermon. The pastor was making a point that sometimes we need to allow ourselves to be immersed in something. In the case of creativity, we marinate in our observations. We allow the time for the observations to coat us, to permeate us, to change us both inside and out. We start to see them in new ways, make new connections, and discover new creative directions. We start to see potential creative ways forward.

It really is at the heart of the description of marinating that you would find at the *Food Network*:

"The purpose of marinating is for the food to absorb the flavors of the marinade or, as in the case of a tough cut of meat, to tenderize."

Biographer David McCullough, author of *John Adams*, talks about marinating in the lives of those he writes about. –

"You've got to marinate your head, in that time and culture. You've got to become them."

We can hover and observe and curate and marinate in a way that we come to a place where we have nearly mastered the content. It is what Anne Graham Lotz was talking about when remembering her dad, Billy Graham, and the way he would preach.

"But when I think of him, I also think of his message because he was immersed in it. Saturated in it. He was his message... a simple man who had responded to God's love by placing his faith in Jesus, receiving the assurance that his sins were forgiven, that he would not perish, but would have everlasting life, simple faith. Faith that matters more than anything else."

Marinating just takes time.

This means that you cannot schedule creativity. It doesn't necessarily happen because you put it on your calendar. Allow yourself to marinate in the car as you drive between tasks. Marinate on walks, as you doze off or as you just wake up. Hover well.

Hovering, whether over waters or rhythms or notes or ideas, is not wasted time. It is sacred space. The Spirit hovers before He speaks. We, too, are invited to linger, to listen, to wait for the moment when the void becomes form. Hovering precedes creation. And when we hover well, we begin to discern the edges. The boundaries that will shape the next act of divine creativity.

Pause and Reflect

We often rush to build, to fix, to speak. But what if the most creative thing we could do right now is hover? What might be revealed if we were still long enough to see the edges of what God is shaping?

Questions to Consider:

Where in your life are you being invited to pause instead of act?

What patterns, needs, or possibilities are emerging as you hover?

What assumptions or distractions might you need to set aside to truly observe?

Are you willing to let stillness shape your next step?

"Around here, however, we don't look backwards for very long. We keep moving forward, opening up new doors and doing new things, because we're curious ... and curiosity keeps leading us down new paths."

Walt Disney

the GENESIS of IDENTIFYING

"Boundaries define us. They define what is me and what is not me. A boundary shows me where I end and someone else begins, leading me to a sense of ownership. Knowing what I am to own and take responsibility for gives me freedom."

From *Boundaries* by Henry Cloud and John Townsend

Explore the Boundaries

And God said, "Let there be light," and there was light. And God saw that the light was good. And God separated the light from the darkness. God called the light Day, and the darkness He called Night. And there was evening and there was morning, the first day.

Genesis 1:3-5

The book of *Genesis* begins with creation. The story tells of God working on the creation of everything we know and see over the course of six days. That is a tight time frame. But what's interesting is that more than half of the time was really spent on exploring and identifying the boundaries. After those three and a half days, the real creativity started. In Genesis, God defines space before He fills it, definition precedes design. We'll trace those boundaries day by day, then explore how limits ignite creativity, from Gehry's acoustics to Pixar's pixels.

Day one – God makes the day to separate the light from the darkness, an act of definition, not division. Not only does He separate them, but He also defines them. The light is Day, and the dark is Night.

Day two – God separates the waters above and the waters below. You may remember from earlier that God was hovering over the chaos of the deep. Chaotic waters were the norm. God called for an expanse to keep waters down here on earth, and in the ancient Near Eastern imagination, the waters that covered us above. God called the waters above – sky, or heavens, or firmament. It was the boundary between the above and below.

Day three – God gathers the waters below and allows land to appear. God defines the boundaries between land and sea. With land defined, food and habitat become imaginable.

With the scaffolding in place, the filling begins.

Without these boundaries, the possibilities of what to create are limitless, and that can keep us from even starting to try. With boundaries, things start to make sense. The amount of light and dark has implications on what can grow. Creating things to live in the water comes with a set of limitations. What will it breathe? How will it move? What can it do, and not do? The same with land. The same with sky and space. And once the field starts filling with players, they begin to influence the creation of each other. Who is predator, and who is prey?

Identifying is the second movement in the creative rhythm: hovering first, then identifying what is, and what will be.

The Architects

Have you ever faced a blank page or an empty canvas, unsure where to begin? That paralysis usually comes when the possibilities feel endless. You don't know where to start because there are too many variables, too many options. We call it "thinking outside the box," but taken to an extreme, it can cause us to freeze up. In real life, money is finite, space is fixed, and resources are limited. Whether you're a kid in school or a Fortune 500 CEO, there are always boundaries to work within.

I spent formative years at the University of Washington, go Huskies! The campus sprawls across 634 acres. If you counted faculty, staff, and students when I was there, it would have rivaled a mid-sized Washington city.

My favorite view on campus came just past Suzzallo Library. On a clear day, Drumheller Fountain lined up perfectly with Mount Rainier, a reminder that good design pays attention to its boundaries and horizons.

Architecture taught me what Genesis soon would: design begins with definition.

Those years trained my eyes for every city I've visited since; from Manhattan's skyscrapers to the old quarters of New Orleans, to the missions of Southern California, from Nairobi's Kibera to the Acropolis. I look for how places are shaped by their limits.

One architect keeps catching my eye: Frank Gehry. I've studied Seattle's *MoPop* from nearly every angle, admired photos of the Guggenheim Bilbao, and stood in awe at Walt Disney Concert Hall in Los Angeles. The swooping lines, the shifting metallic skin, it all seems radically new. But to understand those forms, it helps to understand the constraints that birthed them. In other words, limits made the curves.

Early on, Gehry made a splash with *Easy Edges*, a furniture line defined by its boundaries: low cost, fast to produce, and built from cardboard. Cardboard was everywhere - cheap, ignored. But Gehry saw possibility. It "looked like corduroy, it felt like corduroy, it was seductive," and it could be stacked and die-cut into almost any shape. Working inside those limits, he created pieces so successful he stopped the line to keep from distracting from his architecture. Those $15 – $115 chairs are now collectors' items.

By the late '70s, Gehry's career leapt forward with work on his own house. He and his wife had a tight budget, so he leaned into everyday materials – chain-link fence, corrugated aluminum, inexpensive plywood – and found beauty in their constraints.

> *"Here we are surrounded by material that's being manufactured in unimaginable quantities worldwide... We don't even see it. I noticed and started finding ways to beautify it. I wanted to take the curse off the material."*
>
> **Frank Gehry**

Those experiments formed his creative posture: limitation as liberation. When a project offered no clear limits, he stalled.

"I had a horrible time with it... It's better to have some problem to work on. I think we turn those constraints into action."

Gehry's struggle mirrors the first verses of Genesis. God first shaped space; separating, naming, defining. Boundaries precede brilliance.

Disney Hall is the proof. Brutal acoustic requirements dictated the interior geometry. Those interior boundaries then inspired the now-iconic exterior, form following finely tuned limits. This is not creativity from a blank slate; it's creativity sparked by structure. As Stravinsky put it, "The more constraints one imposes, the more one frees oneself."

What Gehry tapped into was the genesis of boundaries. And architecture isn't the only place where constraints ignite innovation.

Boundaries are not barriers but beginnings.

Every framework – a stage, a page, a budget, a heartbeat –

exists to give shape to freedom. Creativity thrives when it meets resistance; friction generates fire. The first divisions of light and dark, sea and sky, were not confinements but invitations for new life to flourish within their lines. When we honor the edges of our resources, we often discover unexpected beauty inside them.

It is interesting to note that this idea of boxed creativity is not unique to the Bible. Native Americans in the Pacific Northwest tell stories of Raven, the trickster. In one story, Raven opened a box that was off-limits. Inside the box was another box, and another, and another, until the final box held all the light in the universe. Raven released the light into the world's confines so it could serve humanity.

The ancients grasped this. "Necessity is the mother of invention," said Plato. We've drifted from that wisdom. As author and consultant Dan Roberts observes, children see a plain cardboard box as a rocket, castle, or boat. Adults see recycling. Somewhere between childhood and the boardroom, we lost the wonder of working within the box, and the modern obsession with erasing boundaries began.

Where did it begin?

Origin of the Box

In the 1970s, psychologist J.P. Guilford conducted a series of studies on creative thinking. His most famous contribution introduced what we now call the nine-dot puzzle popularized by creativity researchers building on Guilford. Participants were asked to connect nine dots arranged in a square using only four straight lines, without lifting their pencil from the paper.

Only about 20 percent solved it. Most stayed trapped inside the invisible square their minds had drawn around the dots. Guilford concluded that the key to creativity was seeing beyond the boundaries of the box, and thus a cultural metaphor was born.

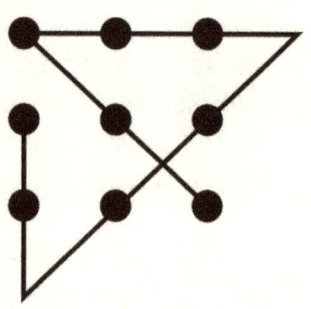

What began as a clever exercise in perception soon became an anthem for innovation. Business leaders seized on the phrase *think outside the box* as a rallying cry for originality. By the 1980s, the mantra had infiltrated classrooms, boardrooms, and brainstorming sessions everywhere. Yet the irony is hard to miss: in trying to escape the box entirely, we abandoned the very framework that makes creativity possible. Simply telling people to "be creative" without defining their field of play rarely produces breakthrough ideas. Instead of freedom, it often leads to frustration.

Pastor Steven Furtick calls this the "if-then mindset;" a kind of creative paralysis born from limitless hypotheticals.

If I had more money, I could make something great.

If I had more time, then I could finally do my best work.

If I had the right team, then I could succeed.

But real life doesn't work that way. None of us have unlimited resources, hours, or help. We live, and create, within boundaries.

Pastor Craig Groeschel describes the same problem in modern terms:

> **"The problem with outside-the-box thinking is there are unlimited options; it's like trying to find something to watch on Netflix or Amazon Prime. Constraints drive creativity. When you have options, you have to make decisions, and decisions drain your energy. You end up living with decision fatigue."**

Psychologists call this the *tyranny of choice* – the illusion that more options equal more freedom. The opposite is true.

Think of the difference between a Michelin-star chef's small tasting menu and *The Cheesecake Factory's* novel-length list of entrées. At the tasting menu, limits sharpen creativity. Each dish is crafted with care, balanced and intentional. At *Cheesecake Factory*, the abundance can feel overwhelming, you could spend twenty minutes just trying to decide between pasta, tacos, or omelets.

Boundaries act like that pared-down menu. They focus the experience and free us to actually enjoy it. Too many options, on the other hand, can paralyze us. Creativity thrives not in endless possibility but in purposeful selection.

In other words, boundaries don't hinder imagination, they protect it. Like the frame around a painting or the rhythm of a song, constraints give creativity its focus and form. And when the frame is right, the picture emerges.

Pop Culture and the Rise of the Box

By the late twentieth century, the box had become a fixture of pop culture, both a symbol of conformity and a challenge to transcend it. Phrases like "collapse the box," "get rid of the box," and "think beyond the box" filled boardrooms, classrooms, and bestselling books.

Figures such as Deepak Chopra and T. D. Jakes championed the call to escape the box altogether,

Boundaries in action

One of my best friends growing up now lives 6,000 miles away and speaks a different language.

He spent most of his life in Seattle and later become a pilot in Spokane. We were close, both relationally and geographically. But for his 20th wedding anniversary, he and his wife decided to take a trip to France. At the time, they had no idea this would lead to exploring their boundaries.

What they found in France was breathtaking: a beautiful country filled with beautiful people. Yet beneath the grandeur of old cathedrals - now serving as tourist attractions, coffee shops, and bookstores - they saw a deeper need. The people of France needed Jesus.

That realization pushed them to test the boundary. They packed up their lives, and moved to France to become missionaries. When they arrived, they didn't know the language. They didn't know anyone there. All they knew was that God had shown them an opportunity, and they chose to take it.

Over time, they grew into their new life. They learned the language, built relationships, and found what they needed to get the job done. Just as God defined light from darkness, my friends stepped into the unknown and discovered where faith's boundaries gave birth to new beginnings.

Now, we stay connected over Zoom, and though the miles between us are great, I remain thankful for their friendship and for their willingness to explore the boundaries.

Their story reminds us that the biggest leaps of faith often begin at the edge of what we know.

equating boundaries with limitation and liberation with unbounded potential. For Chopra, the box represented the conditioned mind, rigid frameworks shaped by culture, habit, and fear. His holistic philosophy invited followers to dissolve those mental walls and awaken to a freer, more intuitive consciousness.

Jakes approached the metaphor from a spiritual and empowerment perspective. His challenge to "invent the world you see inside" reframed the box as both social constraint and personal barrier, a set of inner fears that keep us from living out our divine purpose. Breaking free, in his view, meant embracing faith, courage, and vision to create something transformative.

Popular culture echoed these messages. *The Matrix* imagined freedom from the confines of illusion; *The Catcher in the Rye* rebelled against social expectation; *Dead Poets Society* urged a generation to "seize the day." Each celebrated the act of escape, of breaking boundaries, rejecting structure, and pursuing authenticity at all costs.

Yet not every voice agreed. Malcolm Gladwell offered a subtle correction: "If everyone has to think outside the box, maybe it's the box that needs fixing." His insight reframes the issue, not all boundaries are bad. The real challenge is to discern between those that confine and those that define. Without a box, creativity risks becoming directionless and detached from reality.

The Problem with Jargon

Over time, the phrase *think outside the box* lost its power. Once a spark for innovation, it became corporate shorthand, an empty slogan used to demand originality without offering focus.

The result? Meetings full of ideas but devoid of direction.

Imagine a team asked to brainstorm a new product without any framework, no audience, no budget, no goal. The conversation spirals into wild speculation: flying cars, teleportation, time machines. But without boundaries, none of it can move forward. By contrast, when clear constraints are in place, like a specific market, price point, or need, creativity finds traction.

Worse still, many of our boxes aren't real at all. They're false boundaries, assumptions we mistake for truth. A team says, "That's not how we've always done it," and innovation stalls. A startup avoids remote work because it feels too unfamiliar. A teacher sticks to standardized tests, fearing open-ended learning will fail. In each case, the limitation isn't the box itself, it's our refusal to reimagine it.

The key isn't to destroy the box but to see it clearly. Boundaries can either imprison us or empower us depending on how we use them. The healthiest creativity, whether in business, education, or art, doesn't reject structure; it redefines it.

Ask yourself: *Is this boundary real, chosen, or assumed?*

Outside the Box: Innovation or Chaos?

The call to *think outside the box* can spark innovation - but without structure, it often spirals into chaos. Street artist Banksy captured both the allure and the danger in his famous line: "Think outside the box, collapse the box, and take a f*ing sharp knife to it." It sounds rebellious, even romantic. Yet when every boundary is cut away, creativity can lose its focus and drift into noise.

The truth is, freedom without form is chaos. Creativity needs containment the way water needs a riverbank.

Boundaries do not suppress imagination, they give it energy and direction.

Consider Pixar in its earliest days. The limitations of 1990s computer graphics - slow processors, limited memory, and primitive rendering tools - forced animators to invent new methods within those technical walls. Those constraints shaped the distinctive look of *Toy Story* and laid the foundation for a new era of storytelling. The boundary became the birthplace of innovation.

History offers other lessons. During the dot-com bubble, countless startups pursued grand ideas with no real framework or discipline. Their lack of structure led to spectacular collapse. Meanwhile, companies like Google thrived precisely because they defined clear boundaries. Policies like their "20% Time" rule invited creativity within a structure, freedom framed by purpose. That paradox is what sustained innovation.

The same rhythm appears throughout creative history. Thomas Edison's work was famously iterative, grounded in thousands of experiments. Each test had boundaries, defined parameters, clear questions, measurable results. Those constraints didn't hinder discovery; they made discovery possible. His refinement of the light bulb was not the triumph of chance but of disciplined curiosity.

True creativity, then, is not about escaping the box but redesigning it. It's the art of shaping the container so that what's inside can flourish. The boundaries change, but the principle remains: order first, then creation. It's the same pattern we see in Genesis; light divided from darkness, waters separated from sky, formlessness, then form.

Reframing the Box

What if, instead of erasing the box, we redesigned it? The box isn't a prison for our ideas; it's a framework that gives them form. Boundaries, when rightly drawn, don't limit creativity; they focus it. History's greatest achievements are often the result of working within well-defined constraints.

Consider the sonnet, a poetic form confined by strict rhyme and meter. Within those 14 lines, writers from Shakespeare to Frost discovered endless possibilities.

In music, the 12-bar blues has served as a structure for innovation across genres, from early jazz to modern rock. Its boundaries didn't stifle invention; they made it sing. Likewise, the rules of sustainable architecture: efficiency, reuse, stewardship - have driven some of the most creative design solutions of our time. In every case, the limit becomes the launchpad.

In business, reframing the box means reevaluating goals, resources, and assumptions. A company paralyzed by stagnation might find new momentum by redefining its purpose. Say, committing to sustainability or community impact. Such self-imposed constraints channel creativity rather than choke it. Teams using design thinking follow this same pattern: clearly define the problem, embrace the parameters, and then innovate within them.

Moving Forward

Voices like Deepak Chopra and T. D. Jakes remind us of the ongoing tension between freedom and form. Chopra calls us to dissolve the limits that keep us small; Jakes challenges us to imagine the world that lies within. Both are right, and yet,

Genesis shows us a deeper truth: true creativity doesn't come from escaping boundaries but from working faithfully within them.

To see this in practice, imagine a team tasked with developing a new sustainable product line.

Identify Real Boundaries: They begin by naming genuine limits, using only recyclable materials, maintaining a budget under $100,000.

Embrace Constraints as Opportunities: They treat those restrictions not as obstacles but as creative prompts.

Redesign When Necessary: As the project evolves, they reassess their framework, ensuring each boundary serves the goal rather than hinder it.

That process mirrors divine creativity itself; definition, exploration, and adjustment until the work takes form. Boundaries become not walls but scaffolding for what's next.

As we continue to explore the creative rhythm of Genesis, we'll see this pattern unfold again and again: form leading to fullness, boundary giving rise to connection.

The box isn't the enemy of creativity, it's the birthplace of it.

Studies of Creativity and Boundaries

Modern research continues to confirm what Genesis showed from the start: boundaries don't restrict creativity, they release it.

One fascinating study looked at how boundaries affect exploration. Researchers placed groups of rats in two environments: one enclosed, the other open and boundary-free. The results were surprising. The rats without boundaries moved cautiously, rarely venturing far from their starting point.

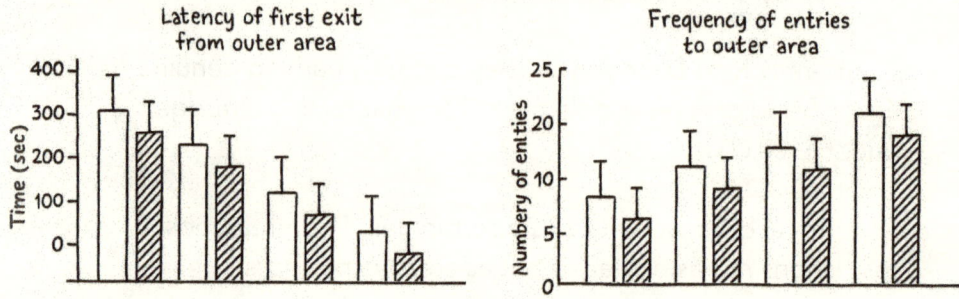

The rats in confined spaces, however, explored more freely and with greater confidence (Ennaceur, 2006). Within structure, they discovered freedom.

A similar pattern appeared on the playground. Landscape architects studied how children played when their environment was either fenced or open. On unfenced playgrounds, children tended to huddle near their teachers. But when a fence was added, when boundaries were visible, the children used the entire space, running and imagining without fear. The presence of boundaries didn't limit play; it liberated it (Maya, 2018).

Physical boundaries are easy to see, but the same truth applies to intellectual and creative ones. Research across education, business, and the arts keeps revealing the same pattern: clear limits encourage innovation.

In higher education, Casper (2013) found that teaching suffers when institutions insist on "outside-the-box" thinking that ignores shared history and culture. The best learning, he discovered, happens when ideas are built inside a framework of community and continuity.

In the workplace, Davis (2013) explored how leaders manage creativity. He found that the most innovative employees weren't those freed from all structure but those who learned to integrate boundaries from other parts of life, especially leisure, where play and problem-solving intersect. The box was not abolished; it was reimagined.

In medical education, Al-Eraky (2015) identified a similar pattern. Students learn best when the process includes clear parameters: a subject, a method, a medium, and a way to measure learning. Those patterns, the academic 'box', create the conditions for new ideas to emerge.

Even the psychology of play supports this truth. Dahl (2007) showed that people often feel more confident and creative when faced with ambiguous or flexible boundaries. Paradoxically, total freedom can cause paralysis, while gentle structure sparks experimentation.

Artists have long intuited what researchers are now proving. George Harrison, staring at a blank page and feeling creatively stuck, imposed a limit on himself: he'd write a song based on the first words he saw in a book. The words were "gently weeps," and the result became one of his most beloved songs, *While My Guitar Gently Weeps*.

The same principle shows up in other studies. Stokes (2014) found that experts, people who know their field deeply, are actually less creative when given no constraints. They tend to repeat what's worked before. But when limits are introduced, they're pushed to think differently, combining familiar tools in unfamiliar ways. Creativity, in other words, thrives inside the toolbox.

Poet and researcher Baer (2014) pointed to the haiku, just three lines, seventeen syllables, as a perfect example. Its tight form demands precision, and that precision becomes the spark of beauty. Restriction doesn't kill expression; it refines it.

Perhaps the clearest affirmation comes from a study commissioned by Red Bull (Winfrey, 2016). When the company interviewed 500 of the most creative people alive, the majority agreed that "thinking inside the box" was critical to their creativity. The most innovative minds didn't reject boundaries; they embraced them.

> An old silent pond...
> A frog jumps into the pond,
> splash! Silence again.
> —Matsuo Basho

Across species, classrooms, studios, and boardrooms, the pattern holds. Boundaries give rise to imagination. They turn chaos into coherence. They mirror the divine rhythm of creation itself, definition first, then design.

We tend to see limits as loss, yet they are often the very scaffolds that hold our purpose steady. A melody needs measures. A painting needs a frame. Even our days are bounded by morning and evening so that meaning can take form inside the hours. The challenge is not to erase boundaries but to explore them, to press against them until they reveal new possibilities.

Practical Takeaways

Define Your Boundaries: Identify your resources, time, and tools. See them as opportunities, not obstacles.

Embrace Constraints: Treat your limits as part of the creative challenge. Ask, "How can I innovate within these lines?"

Reflect on God's Example: Just as God established boundaries before filling creation with life, set your own framework before beginning your next project.

Boundaries are not the end of creativity, they're its beginning.

From the very first day of creation, God wasn't simply dividing light from darkness or sea from sky. He was preparing the world for relationship. Every boundary He set became a meeting place, where light meets dark, land meets sea, and heaven meets earth. Each limit was an invitation for something new to grow, to interact, to depend on something else.

This is the divine rhythm: first form, then fullness. First boundaries, then connection.

The same rhythm plays out in us. When we acknowledge the real constraints of our lives; our time, our resources, our values, we become free to create something meaningful within them. And what we create rarely stands alone. It reaches. It connects. It brings things together that once seemed divided.

God's next movement in Genesis shifts from separation to communion from forming space to filling it. The heavens and earth become home to living things; the rhythms of day and night sustain them; the boundaries of creation become the framework for relationship. Creativity grows not in isolation, but in connection, between ideas, between people, between heaven and earth.

Pause and Reflect

Boundaries are not the end of creativity, they're its beginning.

They remind us where we are, so we can imagine what could be.

Before you shape what's next, pause and consider what God might already be shaping through the limitations around you. Sometimes the very edges we resist become the framework for His most surprising work.

Questions to Consider

What boundaries in your life are inviting - not restricting - your creativity?

Can you recall a time when a constraint led to unexpected clarity or inspiration?

Where might new connections emerge from the structure you've already built?

"To me, there's no creativity without boundaries. If you're gonna write a sonnet, it's 14 lines— so it's solving the problem within the container."

Lorne Michaels

the GENESIS of CONNECTING

> "Creativity is just connecting things.
> When you ask creative people how
> they did something, they feel a little guilty because they didn't really do it,
> they just saw something.
> It seemed obvious to them after a while."
>
> **Steve Jobs**

Make New Connections

Then God said, 'Let us make mankind in our image, in our likeness...'

Genesis 1:26

God saw all that He had made, and it was very good. And there was evening, and there was morning - the sixth day.

Genesis 1:31

After five days of forming and filling, God shifts from constructing environments to cultivating relationships. From ordering space to sharing life, the story shifts from habitat to communion.

The Genesis narrative reaches its crescendo not in spectacle but in relationship; creation's climax is communion. God, speaking in plural, (let us make) creates humanity in His image. This divine us has been the subject of centuries of reflection. Christians see in it the first echoes of the Trinity: Father, Son, and Spirit in communion before time. Others see it as a heavenly court or poetic device. But either way, this plurality in unity is unmistakable, and it's imprinted in us.

To be made in God's image is to be made for relationship. This chapter focuses on the third movement, Connecting, how God brings things into right relationship and how creative work flourishes through interdependence.

And that's precisely what creation reflects. The entire structure of Genesis 1 is deeply relational. Light governs time; land nourishes life; stars mark seasons; humanity is formed not above creation, but within it. Everything depends on something else. Every part belongs.

True creativity mirrors this: when ideas, people, and purposes are in right relationship, something "very good" emerges.

When God calls creation "very good," He isn't declaring it merely functional or beautiful. He's naming its wholeness: its shalom.

Shalom is more than peace. It's completeness. It's everything in right relationship. Rabbi Robert Kahn draws a sharp contrast between the Roman ideal of pax and the Hebrew vision of shalom:

*"One can dictate a peace;
shalom is a mutual agreement.
Peace is a temporary pact;
shalom is a permanent condition.
Peace can be negative
the absence of conflict;
shalom is positive
the presence of flourishing.
Peace can be piecemeal; shalom is whole."*

I've grown to understand that shalom isn't the end of conflict. It's the fullness of connection.

Genesis gives us a picture not of disconnected miracles, but of interwoven purpose. The Creator is not a technician assembling a machine, but an artist weaving a world where everything is connected, light, land, sea, sky, creatures, humans, seasons. Nothing is random. Nothing is isolated.

Creation is a web.

And creativity still works that way. Once the boundaries are identified, God begins connecting, filling spaces with relationships so that each thing serves and is served by another. Boundaries make room for relationship.

In this chapter, we'll explore how divine creativity thrives on connection, and how the best human creativity does too. From ecosystems to innovation labs, from biblical poetry to Seattle's cultural landscape, we'll see how very good comes not from isolated brilliance but from relational design.

This understanding of shalom as a web of relationships - not just the absence of chaos, but the presence of harmony - has shaped not only theology, but also the way artists, inventors, and innovators understand their work.

Growing up in Seattle, I witnessed this firsthand.

The Hotshop

I grew up in Seattle, a city wired for creativity. Microsoft was reshaping how the world thought about computers. Amazon started by selling books and quietly grew into a global engine of commerce. Starbucks turned coffee into community. Even the gray skies seemed to draw out new sounds, giving rise to the grunge movement and its raw, introspective honesty.

But amid all that innovation, no one captured the spirit of connection quite like Dale Chihuly.

Chihuly is one of the most celebrated glass artists in history, but he didn't get there by walking the usual path. In fact, his rise to creative greatness was marked by disruption, first by reinvention, then by tragedy, and finally by a bold reimagining of how art could be made.

He began changing the rules of glass art in the mid-1960s. At the time, most glass artists followed traditional forms: vases, bowls, ornaments. Chihuly was different. He started weaving molten glass into wall hangings. He treated the medium like fabric, letting it sag and ripple with intention. He studied under master glassblowers in Europe, absorbing techniques, but always looking for ways to go beyond what had been done before.

By the early 1970s, he was a rising star. His work was gaining international attention. But in 1976, everything changed.

A car accident left Chihuly blind in one eye. For a glassblower, someone whose work relies on precision, balance, depth perception, it was a career-ending injury. For many, that would have been the end. But for Chihuly, it was the beginning of a different kind of creativity - one that was fundamentally about connection.

He could no longer create glass art alone.
So, he didn't.

Chihuly's pivot from solo mastery to team-based making is a case study in connecting people, materials, color, and process.

He formed a team and began to conduct it, sketching forms, choosing colors, cueing timing and temperature. In a field that prized the lone artisan, he embraced interdependence. "I never thought of the team as a compromise," he said. "I thought of it as an expansion."

Limitation didn't end his creativity. It multiplied it.

He began pulling in inspiration from other disciplines. One of his most groundbreaking series, Baskets, was inspired by slumped Native American baskets he had seen in the Pacific Northwest.

"I saw some beautiful Northwest Coast Indian baskets … I wanted to capture that grace in glass."

To do so, he had to translate the feel of woven cedar and bent reed into the unpredictability of molten glass. It was a cross-medium connection that required experimentation, failure, and flexibility, not just from Chihuly, but from his entire team.

In the Macchia series, the connection came through color. Chihuly woke up one morning and decided he wanted to use all 300 colors in the hotshop. He assigned colors for the inside, a different color for the exterior, and a contrasting color for the rim. Pigments and powders were layered in surprising combinations, purple and chartreuse, orange and sky blue. The results were unpredictable. Every piece had to be discovered, not just made. His team became part of that discovery, interpreting, adjusting, responding.

"Throughout the blowing process," he explained, "colors were added, layer upon layer. Each piece was another experiment. When we unloaded the ovens in the morning, there was the rush of seeing something I had never seen before."

This is more than a story of an artist recovering from injury. It's a story of a man embracing his limitations and using them to open an entirely new model of creativity, one based not on mastery alone, but on mutual trust, risk, dialogue, and connection.

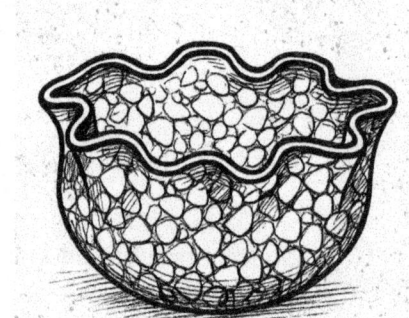

And it worked. Chihuly Studios went on to create some of the most recognizable installations in the world, from the Museum of Glass in Tacoma to the Bellagio in Las Vegas to Chihuly Garden and Glass, which now sits in the shadow of Seattle's Space Needle. Every one of those works is not just a showcase of Chihuly's vision, but of his network of creators, engineers, blowers, designers, riggers, curators, and lighting specialists.

The light didn't just shine through the glass. It shone through the people.

Chihuly's work is beautiful, but more than that, it is communal. And in that sense, it reflects the divine pattern from Genesis. God's act of creation is not a solitary achievement but a movement within divine relationship: "Let us make man in our image." And the world God makes is one of interdependence. Light needs dark. Land needs sea. Creatures need care. And humanity needs relationship, with God, with the earth, and with one another.

Chihuly's hotshop is a parable. Creativity happens in connection. Not just with people, but with ideas, with materials, with surroundings, and with the unexpected limits life brings.

Creativity in Community

It is not good for creativity to be alone. We often think the best work happens when we shut the door, block out the world, and go it alone. But creation doesn't thrive in isolation. It flourishes in relationship.

Even God, mysteriously plural in the creation story, doesn't create in a vacuum. And the world He makes is interconnected by design: ecosystems, relationships, language, beauty. Creativity flows best when it honors that pattern.

We often think of collaboration as a compromise, something to tolerate when we don't have the time, skill, or freedom to do it ourselves. But what if it's where creativity becomes most alive?

Dale Chihuly's studio isn't just a hotshop. It's a theology of trust. Each person adds to the vision. No one can claim the whole. The final work is

Connection in action

While on a learning tour of Nairobi, I had the privilege of meeting the leaders of Kibera Love. Born out of a deep passion to serve, Kibera Love works to uplift people living in Kibera, the second-largest slum in the world.

Kibera, a division of Nairobi, is a place of immense hardship and resilience. The exact population remains uncertain, with estimates ranging from 200,000 to 1 million people. Families live in 12x12 mud-walled huts, and half of the residents face unemployment. Basic services, like electricity, running water, and medical care, are nearly nonexistent. In a community where resources are overwhelmingly limited, two things stand in abundance: rocks and trash.

The Kibera Love team saw a unique opportunity to connect what was available to what was needed. They taught residents to scavenge discarded materials, turning trash into treasure. With creativity, skill, and persistence, the people of Kibera began crafting beautiful pieces of jewelry.

These handcrafted works are now sold online across the globe. The proceeds flow back to Kibera, providing income for the artists and supporting the community in tangible ways. What began with a connection between trash, craftsmanship, and opportunity has blossomed into hope, empowerment, and transformation.

Kibera Love shows that when we connect what's broken to what's possible, God turns scarcity into abundance.

not a pure projection of one mind, it's something more complex, more textured, more human.

When we create in community, we invite surprise. We make room for others to challenge our assumptions, to draw out what we didn't see in ourselves. Collaboration doesn't just help us get things done, it deepens the meaning of what we're doing.

That's the heartbeat of Genesis. Not just that things were made, but that they were made together. That God designed a world where light and dark, land and sea, man and woman, all of it, belong to each other.

So, the next time you're tempted to white-knuckle your way through a project, ask instead:

Who else needs to be part of this?

What ideas am I missing?

Where might connection be the catalyst I need?

You might just find that your best work isn't what you create alone, but what you create together.

Biblical Examples of Creative Community

The building of the Tabernacle in Exodus 31 is one of the clearest and most compelling examples of Spirit-empowered connecting in community.

It's the second time the Spirit of God is mentioned in Scripture, and strikingly, it's not to anoint a prophet or priest or king. It's to equip artists.

> *"See, I have called by name Bezalel... and I have filled him with the Spirit of God, with skill, with intelligence, with knowledge, and with all craftsmanship..."*
>
> **Exodus 31:2–3**

Bezalel is not a preacher or politician. He's a builder, a designer, a creative. And the Spirit's anointing on him is not for speeches or ceremonies, but for the meticulous, collaborative, holy work of crafting a space where heaven meets earth.

He is joined by Oholiab, another Spirit-equipped artisan, and together they don't work alone. The Tabernacle is built through the hands of many: weavers, engravers, metalworkers, woodcarvers, stonesetters, and seamstresses. And even beyond the craftsmen are the donors, ordinary people whose gifts of gold, linen, wood, and thread become part of the sacred architecture. Like Chihuly, Bezalel's creativity wasn't solitary, it was Spirit-filled craftsmanship within community.

It's a divine blueprint for collective creativity.

Every piece of the Tabernacle, from the Ark to the curtains to the lampstands, carries fingerprints from a community of makers. God could have spoken the Tabernacle into existence, but instead He chose to dwell in a space created by His people, shaped through obedience, generosity, and Spirit-filled artistry.

This moment in Scripture affirms that beauty matters, design matters. That the Spirit empowers not just theology, but craftsmanship. It reminds us that creativity is not just decoration, it is participation in God's presence.

In Bezalel's story, we see what happens when creativity is infused with calling, community, and God's Spirit. It's not just good design, it's holy work.

So, whether you're shaping glass, writing code, building a brand, or choreographing a dance, you're standing in a long tradition of Spirit-empowered creators. And you're not meant to do it alone.

If the Tabernacle shows us how God empowers collaboration, Pentecost shows us what happens when that collaboration becomes a community.

When the Spirit descended, it didn't rest on one leader but on all. Tongues of fire. A rush of wind. And suddenly, what had been a fearful, fragmented group becomes a bold, unified movement. The same creative Spirit that hovered over the waters now hovers over a people.

But what happens next is just as powerful.

> *"They devoted themselves to the apostles' teaching and the fellowship, to the breaking of bread and the prayers... And all who believed were together and had all things in common."*

Acts 2:42, 44

The early church didn't just preach differently after the Spirit came, they lived differently. They ate together. They shared possessions. They worshiped, studied, and served as one body. And in doing so, they became a living, breathing expression of God's creativity in relationship.

Theirs was a creativity rooted not in platform or performance, but in presence, in showing up for one another, making space for each other's needs, and building something bigger than any one believer could manage alone.

They didn't have buildings or budgets or blueprints. What they had was unity, hospitality, and shared purpose. And through those connections, the gospel spread like wildfire, not just through sermons, but through how they lived, how they loved, and how they created space for one another.

This kind of creative community isn't flashy. It's faithful.

And it teaches us that some of the most powerful expressions of Spirit-filled creativity look like shared meals, pooled resources, spontaneous generosity, and open doors.

Creativity doesn't always wear a label. Sometimes it looks like a dinner table that keeps adding chairs. Or a home that becomes a refuge. Or a group of believers who choose collaboration over competition.

It's easy to think that the creative Spirit in Acts 2 was about signs and wonders alone. But the real miracle may have been the creation of a community where everyone belonged, and everyone contributed.

The Spirit that hovered over the waters now hovers over a people, forming not a temple of stone but a living temple of souls.

Lessons for Creative Communities

Honoring Every Gift: Every person brings a piece of the divine image to the table.

Fostering Collaboration: Like the Tabernacle builders, we need spaces where people can bring their unique skills to a shared vision.

Encouraging Feedback: Honest, constructive feedback helps refine and elevate creative efforts. Communities provide safe environments for this exchange.

Providing Support: Whether it's emotional encouragement or practical resources, creative communities help sustain individuals through challenges.

Becoming a Creative Hub

To cultivate creativity in your community:

Churches: Host art shows, songwriting workshops, or community-building projects. Celebrate the diverse talents within your congregation.

Families: Foster a culture of creativity at home through collaborative projects, storytelling, or encouraging hobbies.

Workplaces: Encourage brainstorming sessions, interdisciplinary collaboration, and spaces for creative expression.

The goal is not just to gather talent, but to create conditions where creativity becomes contagious.

Be Aware, Be Fearless, Be Flexible

To live creatively within connection requires three postures: awareness, fearlessness, and flexibility.

Be Aware

"It's not what you look at that matters, it's what you see."

Henry David Thoreau

Thoreau was fascinated by trees. As a naturalist and as a writer, trees acted as a moral compass, connected him to times past, and taught him about life and death.

"Talk of mysteries! Think of our life in nature, daily to be shown matter, to come in contact with it, rocks, trees, wind on our cheeks! The solid earth! the actual world! the common sense! Contact! Contact! Who are we? where are we?"

It is his awareness of his surroundings that leads Thoreau to new insights. It is the influence of nature that so many look past, that spoke to Thoreau in ways no person ever could.

This awareness is the same instinct that told Chihuly to explore all the colors in his shop. It is the same awareness that sparked the idea that woven Native baskets could be reproduced in glass, creating art that speaks to people all over the world.

It really brings us back to hovering. Taking the time to see what all around us is. Making the effort to understand all that is within our boundaries.

At times all we see is chaos, formless empty darkness, *tohu va bohu*. But the move of creativity is a movement toward shalom. The wholeness. The completeness. The very good of it all.

Thoreau found shalom at Walden Pond. Chihuly found shalom in simple tools and processes being reimagined. God brought creation to shalom through the interconnectedness of it all.

Awareness is the first act of creation, the willingness to see the chaos not as void, but as potential.

Be Fearless

"A person who never made a mistake never tried anything new."

Albert Einstein

Thomas Edison tried thousands of different materials before finally succeeding in creating a light bulb. One of his assistants is reported to have complained, "All our hard work is in vain. We have gained nothing." Edison replied, "We have come a long way and we have learned a lot. We know that there are 2,000 elements that cannot make a good light bulb."

This is a slight deviation from the creativity of Genesis 1, but it should be a realistic expectation on our part. In Genesis 1 God is doing the creating. In our day to day life it is just us. When we venture into the creative world failure is bound to happen. What becomes an issue is when we view failure as defeat.

Edison was fearless in looking for the right connections to bring light into the world.

Einstein overcame his poor performance as a student, the death of his father, his wife divorcing him and leaving him with the children, and a scientific community that called him crazy. He kept looking for new connections in understanding how the world worked.

For both Edison and Einstein, failure was not final, it was formative.

Chihuly did not quit his passion for glass when he lost sight in one eye, a loss that forced him to reimagine how to create his art. Chihuly charted a new course, connected new inspirations and new techniques and changed the world of glassblowing.

We need two types of fearlessness. One that we need is a dedication to moving forward, regardless of the setbacks. And a second that takes risks making connections that may have never been made before.

Be Flexible

"Great things are done by a series of small things brought together."

Vincent van Gogh

Awareness combined with fearlessness should open us up to new paths and new solutions. This is a second deviation that we make because we are not God. God can step into chaos and is able to know every decision that needs to be made to get the best possible results, we cannot. We come to chaos, or a problem, or an inspired thought with our own expectations and our own baggage. What we need to be is flexible.

Van Gogh was a self-taught artist. In his early years van Gogh learned his art by copying prints and reading drawing manuals and books. He hovered over the art world. His early goal was to master black and white before moving to color. He found his inspiration all around him in landscapes and still lifes. Over time, as his prowess grew, so did his depression, and his art became a means of channeling that depression. He also expanded from drawing to watercolors and lithographs. A move to Paris shifted van Gogh's art into brighter color palettes and impressionistic painting. He also found inspiration in Japanese prints that favored dark outlines. Later in life, van Gogh moved in with Gauguin and they began to influence and change each other. Van Gogh was painting from memory, moving away from realism.

Throughout his life, van Gogh is seen shifting and flexing with his surroundings. His palettes changed, his mediums changed, and much of it was due to how he was changing. Chihuly is also a great example of being flexible with creativity. As his physical ability to work with glass changed so did his art. New creativity can be sparked by new boundaries.

Creative Doesn't Necessarily Mean "New"

Creativity rarely invents from nothing; it reimagines what already exists. Most often, it means new ideas, new observations, new connections. These ideas, observations, and connections require someone to have gone before us. Or something to strike our imagination.

A falling apple exposes gravity.

A new technology hints at new applications.

A particular cloud sparks an idea.

The art of a friend moves you to a new expression of your own art.

So much of creativity is seeing new connections where others have not, building on good ideas and moving them toward great. Leveraging these connections is not the easy way; it is the way. Just as creation weaves existing elements into new forms, our own creativity often depends on reimagining what already is.

Austin Kleon wrote a bestseller about it called *Steal Like an Artist*. In the book, Kleon proposes that no creativity is original and that all ideas stem from other ideas.

Creativity thrives on connections between ideas, disciplines, people, and moments. Whether sparked by a conversation, a memory, a museum, or a melody, creativity flourishes when we see how things are linked. But connection alone isn't enough. To move from spark to substance, something more is required: investment, commitment, patience, and the willingness to give yourself fully to the work that's calling you forward.

Pause and Reflect

Some connections come easily. Others require time, trust, and a deeper level of attention. But once made, they open the door to something more lasting, an investment of time, heart, and imagination.

Questions to Consider

What recent connections -
between people, ideas, or experiences -
have sparked your curiosity?

How might these connections
invite you to go deeper?

What are you being called to invest in more fully?

Are you nurturing surface-level ideas,
or moving toward something more intentional?

"Nothing is original. Steal from anywhere that resonates with inspiration or fuels your imagination. Devour old films, new films, music, books, paintings, photographs, poems, dreams, random conversations, architecture, bridges, street signs, trees, clouds, bodies of water, light and shadows. Select only things to steal from that speak directly to your soul. If you do this, your work (and theft) will be authentic. Authenticity is invaluable; originality is non-existent. And don't bother concealing your thievery - celebrate it if you feel like it. In any case, always remember what Jean-Luc Godard said: 'It's not where you take things from - it's where you take them to.'"

Jim Jarmusch

the GENESIS of INVESTING

"I began by tinkering around with some old tunes I knew. Then, just to try something different, I set to putting some music to the rhythm that I used in jerking icecream sodas at the Poodle Dog. I fooled around with the tune more and more until at last, lo and behold, I had completed my first piece of finished music."

Duke Ellington

Invest Yourself

Then God said, 'Let us make man in our image, after our likeness. And let them have dominion over the fish of the sea and over the birds of the heavens and over the livestock and over all the earth and over every creeping thing that creeps on the earth.'

So God created man in His own image, in the image of God He created him; male and female He created them.

Genesis 1:26–27

The sixth day of creation holds a unique and climactic place in the Genesis account. After five days of divine activity, separating, gathering, naming, and filling, God makes a stunning declaration: "Let us make man in our image, after our likeness." This moment signals a profound shift.

No longer is God simply forming habitats and populating them with living things. Now, God crafts something in His own image. The culmination of creation is not a mountain, a star, or a lion. It is a human being, formed in the likeness of God and imbued with divine purpose.

This creation account was revolutionary.

It stood in stark contrast to the pagan myths of its time, which often relegated humans to the status of disposable servants to capricious gods. In Egyptian myth, humans were formed from the tears of Ra. In Babylonian tradition, they were made from the blood of a defeated god. In these stories, human life is accidental, even expendable. Genesis offers something startlingly different: God made humanity in His image, not to serve divine whims, but to bear divine glory.

This bold declaration shaped a new narrative of purpose. It wasn't just a theological claim, it was a cultural disruption.

In a world where most religions taught that humans were pawns, Genesis taught that humans were partners. Image-bearers. Co-creators. Trustees of the earth. Once God connects the world in right relationship, He invites image-bearers to invest in it, stewarding and developing what's been entrusted. This changes everything about how we view ourselves, our work, and our creative calling.

Humanity is not the product of indifference. We are not here by accident. We are the result of intentional, loving, and personal investment by a Creator who saw fit to place His likeness within us. And if God invests Himself in creation, what does that mean for us? It means that true creativity always involves investment, an offering of ourselves for the sake of something new, something beautiful, something that bears fruit.

This chapter focuses on the fourth movement, Investing: giving time, attention, resources, reputation, and risk to what God has called us to make.

To be made in the image of God is not merely to possess reason or free will, but to share in the divine impulse to shape, to nurture, to give, to risk, and to build.

Just as God spoke, separated, saw, and blessed, we too are invited to act, discern, and bless through what we create.

The Image of God

Theologian Scot McKnight describes the image of God using the Greek word eikon. To bear God's image, he writes, is "to be one designed to love God, self, and others and to represent God by participating in God's rule in this world." In Genesis, the image of God is not a title bestowed but a responsibility entrusted. Humanity is not created to observe God's work from a distance, but to participate in it.

This stands in sharp contrast to the surrounding ancient myths. In many creation stories of the ancient world, humans exist to serve divine needs or absorb divine frustration. Genesis tells a different story. God creates humanity not as expendable servants, but as representatives. God invests Himself in humanity by sharing His own likeness, placing His image within us as a calling rather than a privilege.

The story begins in chaos. The earth is tohu va-vohu, formless and empty. Over six days, God brings order, rhythm, and life. On the sixth day, that creative movement reaches its climax. Humanity is formed in God's tselem (image) and demuth (likeness), not as an afterthought, but as the culmination of

God's creative investment.

Tselem: The Image of Order

Tselem reflects God's capacity to bring order where there was none. It is not simply a trait we possess, but a pattern we are meant to reflect. God does not eliminate chaos by force. He shapes it. He names it. He gives it structure and purpose.

To bear God's image, then, is to participate in that same work. It is to stand faithfully in the midst of uncertainty and bring clarity, care, and intention. In a world that often feels fragmented and unstable, choosing order over disorder, faithfulness over reaction, and responsibility over retreat is itself a creative act.

The image of God is not abstract theology. It is lived investment. God does not create at a distance, and neither are we called to shape the world without cost. To bear His image is to invest ourselves in the work of ordering, tending, and sustaining what He has made.

Demuth: The Echo of Likeness

If tselem speaks to structure and order, demuth speaks to relationship. It is the likeness that allows communion, the resonance between Creator and creature. Demuth is not sameness; it is correspondence. Humanity is not made equal to God, but capable of responding to Him.

God does not simply shape humanity and step away. He draws near. He entrusts Himself. To create in likeness is to invite relationship, and relationship always carries risk. God invests not only power, but presence. He places His image in beings who can choose, resist, love, and wander. That vulnerability is not a flaw in creation; it is the cost of communion.

To bear God's likeness is to be capable of relationship, with God, with others, and with the world itself. It means our creativity is never merely technical or efficient. It is personal. It carries intention, care, and responsibility. We do not simply make things; we enter into relationship with what we make and with those it will affect.

This is why creativity always costs more than effort. It costs attention. It costs trust. It costs willingness to stay connected even when the work becomes difficult or the outcome uncertain. Demuth calls us not just to build structures, but to remain present within them.

In a world that rewards distance, speed, and detachment, bearing God's likeness means choosing proximity. It means staying invested when it would be easier to walk away. God does not create and abandon. He remains with His creation, sustaining it, blessing it, and calling it good.

To reflect God's likeness, then, is to practice creative faithfulness. It is to invest ourselves relationally in the work we begin, trusting that what grows from that investment may exceed our control but not God's care.

The Performer

Often, you don't know the work that goes into making something great. My dad loved to tell people he went to school with Mary Hart. They both attended Augustana Academy in

Sioux Falls, SD, and she became famous as the host of Entertainment Tonight. Her co-anchor? John Tesh.

Tesh was known as a talking head, reading celebrity birthdays. But behind the scenes, he was a musician with six music Emmys, two Grammy nominations, three gold records, seven PBS specials, and eight million records sold. Despite his success in television, music was his passion.

When PBS passed on his pitch for a musical TV special, Tesh decided to invest himself, literally. He envisioned filming at Red Rocks Amphitheater with the Colorado Symphony. With no funding, he and his wife mortgaged their home, eventually borrowing $1.2 million to make it happen.

Their gamble paid off. PBS aired the special, and over the years, it raised more than $20 million for public television. Tesh didn't just invest money, he risked reputation, comfort, and future to bring his vision to life.

Tesh's story reminds us that investment is not always rational. It's sacrificial. It's risky. But it is often the crucible where great creativity is born. He believed that his work had value, and he backed that belief with action.

Tesh's story mirrors God's own creative risk, investing fully. Yet he trusted the process enough to proceed anyway.

The Living Art of Marina Abramovic

Marina Abramović, the grandmother of performance art, also invested herself completely. Born in Belgrade, Yugoslavia, she transitioned from painting to performance art to explore human connection. Her work often pushed her body to the brink, exploring themes of trust, endurance, and vulnerability.

In 2010, her exhibit The Artist Is Present at MoMA featured her silently sitting at a table, inviting viewers to sit across from her. One day, her former partner and collaborator Ulay appeared. They hadn't spoken in 20 years. Their silent reunion was profoundly moving.

Abramović didn't just create art. She became the art. Her performance illustrates the emotional intensity that comes when an artist invests their entire being.

She once said, "The function of the artist is to ask questions, not provide answers." Her vulnerability became the question. Her presence was the canvas. Her pain became the paint. Her work challenges the modern myth that detachment is strength. Instead, she shows us the beauty and courage of total investment.

Whether through money or vulnerability, these artists remind us that creation always demands skin in the game.

Investing Against the Odds

History is filled with people who risked comfort for calling. Great creativity often requires personal investment:

- Jeff Bezos left a high-paying job to start Amazon in his garage.

- Vera Wang walked away from corporate security to design wedding dresses.

- Fred Smith, CEO of FedEx, gambled the company's last $5,000 in Vegas to make payroll. An apocryphal yet enduring story.

Even artists literally paint themselves into their work:

- Caravaggio as Goliath in David with the Head of Goliath.

- Michelangelo as flayed skin in The Last Judgment.

- Toulouse-Lautrec in the background of Au Moulin Rouge.

Actors take this to extremes with method acting:

- Brando lived in a hospital for *The Men*.

- De Niro drove a cab for *Taxi Driver*.

- Gaga stayed in character for

Investment in action

Preshan de Visser grew up in Sri Lanka, a nation torn apart by decades of civil war. Extremist groups had targeted the country's youth with promises of justice, equity, and prosperity. Yet instead of hope and healing, these young people received only violence, exploitation, and an ever-widening gap between the rich and the poor.

Into this brokenness, he invested his life. He observed a pattern: while moderate societies often rely on adults to lead change, gangs and extremist movements always target children. Preshan saw an opportunity to reclaim the youth, not as risks, but as key agents for sustainable peace.

"We don't focus on youth because we see them as a risk," Preshan explains. "We invest in youth because we see them as the linchpin for sustainable peace and national transformation."

In 2009, Preshan founded Sri Lanka Unites, the largest youth movement for reconciliation in the country. Built on principles of hope, healing, and unity, it inspires young people to lead communities out of conflict and into peace. Today, Sri Lanka Unites includes over 25,000 members, representing every district of the nation.

The impact of Preshan's investment continues to ripple across Sri Lanka and beyond. Sri Lanka Unites proves that investing in young people is not just an act of hope, it is an investment in a brighter, more peaceful future for all.

Like the Creator investing His image in humanity, Preshan's investment transformed what was once chaos into hope.

House of Gucci, for 18 months.

- DiCaprio slept in animal carcasses for *The Revenant*.

- Jamie Foxx glued his eyes shut to play *Ray Charles*.

Each of these examples reveals a truth we glimpse in Genesis itself: creation always costs something.

A Call to Create

From the very beginning, God reveals Himself not first as a judge, a warrior, or a lawgiver, but as a Creator. The opening line of Scripture is not a command or a rule, but a work of art: "In the beginning, God created …" Creation is God's first self-disclosure, and it is through this act that we begin to understand who He is and, by extension, who we are.

To be made in the image of this Creator is to be made for making, for shaping, for bringing forth. Creativity is not reserved for the elite few, painters, poets, musicians. It is the birthright of every person fashioned by God. Whether you are a teacher designing a lesson plan, a parent inventing bedtime stories, a mechanic diagnosing an engine, or a neighbor planting a garden, if you are shaping something new in response to the life you've been given, you are creating.

You are not merely permitted to create. You are invited. You are called.

Embracing the Call

This call to create is not always comfortable. It often shows up in the void, those moments of uncertainty, loss, or longing when the world feels formless and empty. But just as God hovered over the waters of chaos and brought forth light, so too are we invited to move toward the chaos with hope. We don't wait for perfect conditions. We begin, as God did, by speaking light.

Embracing the call to create means joining God in His ongoing work to restore, redeem, and renew. It means participating in His mission, not just by preaching or teaching, but by designing, building, organizing, healing, feeding, painting, parenting, and problem-solving. It is an act of faith to make something beautiful in a broken world.

When we create, we don't just reflect God's image, we extend His love. We declare that beauty still matters. That newness is possible. That hope is alive.

The call to create is an invitation to bring order to chaos, beauty to brokenness, and hope to despair. Whether we create through art, relationships, problem solving, or innovation, we mirror God's divine creativity.

> *"For we are God's handiwork, created in Christ Jesus to do good works, which God prepared in advance for us to do."*
>
> **Ephesians 2:10**

Living as an Image-Bearer

Living as an image-bearer means responding to God's invitation to create with the same spirit of intention, beauty, and sacrifice we see in Genesis. It involves understanding who we are, how we act, who we involve, and where we belong. Here are four dimensions of that life:

Identity: Know Who You Are

You are not an accident. You are not disposable. You are not a machine. You are a bearer of the divine image, designed with purpose and called to participate in God's redemptive creativity. Your unique wiring, experiences, and passions are not incidental, they are clues to how God intends to work through you.

Action: Begin Creating

Start small. You don't need to create a masterpiece overnight. Begin with intentional acts of creativity, whether writing a song, planning a meal, crafting a lesson plan, or offering a word of encouragement. Creation flows from doing.

Reflect on your gifts. What have you been given? What brings you joy or energy? How can you use those passions to reflect God's goodness in the world?

Involve God in your process. Pray. Listen. Invite His Spirit into the work. Your creativity isn't just self-expression, it's participation in something bigger.

Relationships: Stay Connected

You were not made to create in isolation. Find your cheerleaders, people who believe in your calling and show up when the work gets hard. Surround yourself with those who challenge and encourage you.

Consistency also matters. When people look at your work,

do they recognize your values, your voice? Be authentic in your creativity. Let your character shine through.

Community: Invite Others In

Even the most personal creative acts are influenced by those around us. Editors, producers, mentors, and audiences all help shape the work. When we welcome others into the creative process, we enrich the outcome and amplify its reach.

True investment means giving of ourselves for the sake of something that will bless others. And often, the deepest joy in creating comes when our work becomes a gift to the community around us.

What Next?

How Do We Reflect the Image of God?

This should be good news. Especially for anyone who has never thought of themselves as creative. A creative God, in the most creative act ever accomplished, made you in His image. Not as an afterthought. Not as a utility. But as a bearer of His likeness. That alone should free us from hesitation and invite us forward with confidence and joy.

Across these chapters, we've traced a pattern woven into creation itself: chaos is named, boundaries are set, connections are formed, and investment is made. These are not just divine actions. They are invitations. Because we are created in God's image, we are able, and called, to wield these same movements in our own lives and work.

But reflecting God's image goes beyond creativity alone. Genesis 1 reminds us that every person bears that image. Which means every life carries weight. Every voice deserves dignity. Every act of creation exists within a wider human community. To create faithfully is not only to make something new, but to do so with care for those it will affect.

So the question becomes personal.

What part of your creation carries you?

When people encounter your work, do they sense presence, intention, integrity? Voice is formed over time. It emerges through consistency, faithfulness, and the courage to remain yourself even as the work evolves. People come to recognize us not because our work is perfect, but because it is honest.

And you are not meant to do this alone.

Creative courage rarely grows in isolation. It needs encouragement, challenge, accountability, and support. Find the people who believe in what you are making. Invite them into the process. Let them carry part of the weight when the cost feels high.

Because investment is never merely individual. Creation has always been communal. Even God's first creative declaration was spoken in the plural: Let us make. Every meaningful work draws from shared influence and shared effort, whether through mentors, collaborators, editors, audiences, or friends who refuse to let us quit.

You were made in the image of a Creator who hovered, separated, connected, and invested. And so you are called to create with intention, integrity, and sacrifice. But investment is not the final act.

At some point, the work must be carried forward through time, tested, refined, released, and returned to again and again. Greatness does not come from striving for perfection. It grows through patience, perseverance, and faithfulness over the long haul.

That is where we turn next.

Because what God calls very good is rarely finished all at once. Sometimes, very good is still coming.

Pause and Reflect

Deep work demands deep investment. And that kind of investment will always cost something. But the cost of not investing, of holding back, is often greater. What new act of creation might God be waiting to begin through your willingness to invest?

Questions to Consider:

What creative work have you invested in that still needs tending?

Where are you holding back, and why?

What would it look like to invest more fully - emotionally, spiritually, practically?

Is there a cost you're being asked to trust God with?

"Write what you know."

Mark Twain

the GENESIS of PERSISTING

"Great things are done by a series of small things brought together"

Vincent van Gogh

Very Good May Still Be Coming

26 Then God said, "Let us make man in our image, after our likeness. And let them have dominion over the fish of the sea and over the birds of the heavens and over the livestock and over all the earth and over every creeping thing that creeps on the earth."

27 So God created man in his own image, in the image of God He created him; male and female he created them.

28 And God blessed them. And God said to them, "Be fruitful and multiply and fill the earth and subdue it and have dominion over the fish of the sea and over the birds of the heavens and over every living thing that moves on the earth."

29 And God said, "Behold, I have given you every plant yielding seed that is on the face of all the earth, and every tree with seed in its fruit. You shall have them for food. 30 And to every beast of the earth and to every bird of the heavens and to everything that creeps on the

> earth, everything that has the breath of life, I have given every green plant for food." And it was so.
>
> **31** And God saw everything that he had made, and behold, it was very good. And there was evening and there was morning, the sixth day.
>
> **Genesis 1:26–31**

This chapter focuses on the fifth movement, Persisting: the disciplined, iterative work that carries creation from 'good' toward 'very good.'

In Genesis 1, we witness the pinnacle of divine creativity. Each day, God forms, fills, and blesses creation, and at the end of each day, He declares it "good." But on Day 6, something extraordinary happens. With the creation of humanity, made in God's image and entrusted with stewardship, God declares the work "very good".

That phrase very good is more than a casual upgrade from good. It signals completion, harmony, and divine satisfaction. It's the Hebrew expression *tov me'od*, a profound acknowledgment of completeness, harmony, and purpose. The crescendo of creation is reached not in stars or seas, but in us, image-bearers who are called to mirror God's creative nature.

In Hebrew, tov me'od captures both fullness and movement, goodness that continues unfolding. In that sense, very good may still be coming. God's declaration wasn't a period; it was a comma - an invitation to ongoing participation.

The structure of Genesis 1 suggests a movement from chaos to order, from separation to connection, from formation to fullness. Humanity's creation is the final flourish, the point at which the Artist steps back, sees the whole canvas, and calls it very good.

This declaration invites us to consider what it means to do work that is not just technically good, but deeply integrated, purposeful, and aligned with the Creator's vision. Very good is not about flawlessness; it is about faithful fulfillment. Faithful fulfillment acknowledges process as progress, work that aligns with purpose, not perfection. It's about seeing something completed with care, coherence, and relational harmony. In the biblical sense, "very good" carries a wholeness that reflects the Creator's joy.

In Hebrew thought, this vision of completeness finds another word, *shalom* - not mere absence of defect, but the presence of harmony, fruitfulness, and right relationship.

Think of a meal carefully prepared and shared, not because it's gourmet, but because it nourishes and brings people together.

Think of a poem, a project, a painting that resonates, not for its technical perfection, but for its truth. This is the essence of very good. It is not about impressing. It's about embodying.

This also means that very good is not an end in itself. It is a beginning. God creates humanity and immediately blesses them and gives them a mission, to be fruitful, multiply, fill, subdue, and steward. The "very good" of Day 6 becomes the launchpad for meaningful creative action. And that calling, to create faithfully within the world God made, has inspired countless artists.

> *"All humans were made in God's image, so I try to respect the gift of creativity by letting The Truth remain my primary inspiration."*
>
> **Prince**

Day 6 teaches us that great work requires investment, intention, and a willingness to build upon what has come before. It is the culmination of persistence and purpose. The path to "very good" is paved with work that keeps going when good feels like enough.

The Athlete

For me, the idea of "very good" is not abstract. I have watched it form slowly, through repetition, over time.

My cousin's son, Kyrie Irving, wrote a sentence on the wall of his closet when he was still a kid: *I will be in the NBA.* Years later, on the day he was drafted, he showed that same sentence to his dad. The words had not changed. The years between them had.

What happened in those years is the part most people never get to see.

I saw Kyrie shooting hoops after everyone else went inside. The sound of a basketball on concrete long after the sun had dropped. Free throws taken when there was no scoreboard, no referee, no crowd. Just repetition. Miss. Adjust. Try again.

This is what persisting looks like.

In Genesis 1, God does not declare creation "very good" after the first act of brilliance. Day by day, the work continues.

Light is good. Land is good. Life is good. But "very good" comes only after the long arc of forming, filling, and blessing is complete.

Persistence is the bridge between good and very good.

Athletic discipline reveals this truth with unusual clarity. You cannot rush formation. You cannot shortcut repetition. The body tells the truth every time. Skill is not gifted in a moment; it is cultivated over years. Very good takes time.

Genesis tells us that humanity was created in God's image and given dominion. That word is often misunderstood. Dominion is not domination. It is stewardship. It is learning the limits of what you've been given and committing to tend it faithfully.

That stewardship is rarely glamorous. It looks like staying after practice. It looks like doing the same thing again when no one is watching. It looks like honoring the gift enough to keep showing up.

Persistence itself is an act of creation. To return to the work day after day is to participate in the same rhythm we see in Genesis, where order emerges through patience, care, and sustained effort.

"Very good" is not about flawlessness or uninterrupted success. It is about faithfulness over time. It is about stewarding a gift until it reaches maturity, not because it is perfect, but because it has been shaped with intention and care.

To be faithful with our gifts is to exercise dominion.

Not domination, but creative stewardship.

Very Good vs. Perfect

> *"Have no fear of perfection - you'll never reach it."*
>
> **Salvador Dalí**

Perfection, in Scripture, belongs to God alone. Our task is to pursue *tov me'od*, faithful, wholehearted work.

Genesis makes it clear: very good is not perfect. In fact, the very good doesn't last long. Adam and Eve decide they know better than God, and Eden unravels. But the creative goal for us was never perfection. That's a mirage. "Very good" is what we strive for, our best possible stewardship of the gifts we've been given.

In the biblical imagination, "very good" includes both form and function. It is beauty with purpose, excellence rooted in flourishing. The Hebrew word tov already carries the sense of goodness, and me'od intensifies it, turning it up to its highest degree. So, God's declaration is more than an aesthetic review. It is a celebration of harmony, of potential, of a creation capable of sustaining life and generating new life.

"Very good" means fitting, complete, and alive with possibility. It's not static. It moves forward. It invites co-creation.

Consider some modern examples of this dynamic:

Vincent van Gogh only sold one painting during his lifetime. Today, his work sells for tens of millions. He completed over 1,000 works before his death. He didn't achieve public recognition in his lifetime, but his work was undeniably very good. Filled with expression, emotion, and vibrant beauty that still resonates.

Likewise, Oprah Winfrey was fired from her first job and raised in extreme poverty. She later reflected: "It's about releasing any notions of perfection. Progress is the goal, progress toward a space where you feel more whole and complete." Her very good came not through flawlessness but through faithfulness to her calling.

J.K. Rowling, rejected by 12 publishers, manually typed out copies of her 90,000-word manuscript because she couldn't afford a printer. One publisher's daughter read it, and changed literary history. Rowling has said: "Perfection is not necessary to make a real and lasting difference to other people's lives."

Each of these creators reminds us that 'very good' emerges not from perfection but perseverance, staying faithful through obscurity, setbacks, and uncertainty. Their stories prove that very good work is rarely recognized in its own time, but always grounded in faithfulness.

Very Good Takes Time

Just as creation unfolded over six days, the most enduring work unfolds through time. God could have stopped creating on day three and still have crafted a world better than anything we could imagine. But He didn't. God continued, envisioning a "very good" that required persistence and progression.

Freddie Mercury's masterpiece, "*Bohemian Rhapsody*," was 15 years in the making. Starting with early ideas in the 1960s, Mercury refined and expanded the song over time. In 1975, Queen spent weeks rehearsing and recording, with some sections requiring 180 separate overdubs. Time itself became part of its greatness.

Animated films also illustrate this principle. Walt Disney's *Sleeping Beauty* took years to complete, as animators meticulously modeled their drawings on live-action performances to achieve unparalleled realism.

Michael Crichton's *Jurassic Park* was another labor of love, requiring

Very Good in action

Bolorhuu Ligden is the Founder and Executive Director of Asia Leadership Development. Bolorhuu comes from Mongolia, a place that once felt as distant from my world as any place could be. Yet through our friendship, Bolorhuu has opened my eyes to the remarkable possibilities that come when we commit to pushing toward "very good."

His story begins at a pivotal moment in history. As his website describes it:

"In 1990, when Communism ended in Mongolia, the country began to open up to the world ... At that time, there were only four (4) known Mongolian Christian believers. Soon afterward…many Christian groups started entering the country and working among the Mongolian people to share the Good News of Jesus Christ."

The transformation has been astounding. Christianity in Mongolia has grown from 4 believers to more than 100,000. Today, there are over 500 churches across the country, and Christians are actively serving in positions of political leadership, influencing their nation and beyond.

This journey has not been quick or easy. It represents a commitment to the principle of "very good", the belief that the effort to build, grow, and sustain something meaningful is worth the time and dedication required.

It reminds us that extraordinary results often emerge when we refuse to settle for "good enough." Mongolia's transformation is a testament to the power of perseverance, vision, and unwavering hope.

Their story reminds us that 'very good' rarely comes overnight, it's born from faithful persistence that mirrors God's own creative patience.

years of scientific research and writing. The result was a novel so compelling that it spawned a blockbuster film series that continues to captivate audiences decades later.

Like God's creation unfolding over six days, these masterpieces - *Bohemian Rhapsody, Sleeping Beauty, Jurassic Park* - show that the most enduring work is born of patience and persistence. Enduring creativity, like divine creation, matures through persistence and patience.

Very Good is Work

I hesitate to draw this parallel too closely, but in Genesis 2:2 we find this:

> *"By the seventh day God had finished the work he had been doing; so on the seventh day he rested from all his work."*

I've heard it said that to understand what it means for God to rest, we should think of it as God taking up residence in His creation, like a king taking a seat on his throne.

Like Kyrie Irving practicing day and night, many creative individuals work tirelessly at what others might perceive as effortless. Comedy, for example, often looks deceptively easy.

The Relentless Work of Steve Martin

Effortless joy often hides disciplined labor. Steve Martin is one of the funniest people I've ever watched. His humor seems so natural and effortless that you'd think hanging out with him would be nonstop laughs. However, Martin tells a different story. In an interview on NPR's *Fresh Air*, he reflected on his career:

> *"I did stand-up comedy for 18 years. Ten of those years were spent learning, four years were spent refining, and four years were spent in wild success."*
>
> **Steve Martin**

Greatness often looks effortless, but behind every 'very good' is the grind of unseen labor.

Martin is known for writing, testing, rewriting, memorizing, tweaking, and sweating every detail to achieve that sense of effortlessness. The life of a top-tier comedian can be monotonous. As an undergraduate at Long Beach State College, Martin majored in philosophy. Inspired by Descartes' "I think, therefore I am," he approached comedy from the ground up, deconstructing and rebuilding it.

Martin's success was no accident. It was the product of meticulous preparation and relentless work. Effortless art is built on years of unseen effort."

The Discipline of Improv

Another example of the work behind seemingly effortless creativity is improvisation. Tina Fey is one of the greatest writers and performers to emerge from *Saturday Night Live*. A talented actor, author, and screenwriter, Fey got her start in improv.

Despite its reputation for spontaneity, improv thrives on structure and preparation. In her book *Bossypants*, Fey outlines her "Rules for Improvisation," which include:

- Always agree and say "yes."

- Make statements instead of asking questions.

- Focus on your scene partner.

- There are no mistakes.

Just as God brought order from chaos, improv thrives not despite structure but because of it.

Improv relies on participants working together within shared rules to reach "very good." Even improv, an art form that seems boundless, thrives on structure. Just as Genesis shows, boundaries don't limit creativity; they give it shape.

When we pursue very good, we are not trying to impress God or imitate perfection. We are partnering with Him in the ongoing act of cultivation, of shaping, refining, and releasing beauty into the world.

What Next?

What keeps you from continuing?

Maybe it's fear of failure. Or the exhaustion that sets in after trying and not seeing results. Maybe it's the voice that says "good enough" is safer than risking disappointment. But here's the truth: very good isn't reserved for the famous or the flawless. It's for the faithful.

Pursuing very good means embracing the long haul. It means showing up again and again. Not because it's easy, but because it's worth it. Very good requires courage to endure criticism, humility to accept edits, and wisdom to know when to keep refining and when to release.

Revisit

Refine

Rethink

Reclaim

The rhythm of creation continues through your work.

When God finished creation, He called it very good. Not perfect. Not untouchable. But complete, beautiful, and ready to live.

You may never paint a Starry Night or write Bohemian Rhapsody, but you bear the image of a God who does great work, and calls you to do the same.

That's the invitation: to keep showing up. To refine, to revisit, to release. Not because the work is easy, but because it's worth it. Creativity done in faithfulness will stretch and surprise you. But when it is honest, good, and offered with love, it lives. And sometimes, it even grows into something more than you imagined.

Let it live.

Pause and Reflect

Very good isn't a finish line. It's a moment of release. A recognition that your work, once shaped with care, is ready to go out and bless others. Can you trust it to live, even if it grows beyond your control?

Questions to Consider:

What does "very good" look like in your current season?

Where in your creative life are you tempted to settle for "good enough"?

What part of your work is ready to be released, even if it's not perfect?

How have you seen God use something you've let go of?

*"It's very easy to get a break.
It's very hard to be good enough.
Most of us think about impressing others
at the important moment.
But that's all about appearances.
Instead, focus on constant improvement
and be the real deal.
As Jose Narosky said:
'Many are the varnish.
Few are the wood.'"*

Jerry Seinfeld

the GENESIS of RELEASING

"To my mind one does not put oneself in place of the past, one only adds a new link."

Paul Cézanne

Let It Live

28 And God blessed them. And God said to them, "Be fruitful and multiply and fill the earth and subdue it, and have dominion over the fish of the sea and over the birds of the heavens and over every living thing that moves on the earth." 29 And God said, "Behold, I have given you every plant yielding seed that is on the face of all the earth, and every tree with seed in its fruit. You shall have them for food. 30 And to every beast of the earth and to every bird of the heavens and to everything that creeps on the earth, everything that has the breath of life, I have given every green plant for food." And it was so. 31 And God saw everything that He had made, and behold, it was very good. And there was evening and there was morning, the sixth day.

Genesis 1:28-31

Here, God brings creation to its threshold, a moment when it must now be released. God sees that it is very good and knows that it is time. Those familiar with the next chapter of Genesis know this is not the end of the story, but for now, we linger here.

This is a profound turning point. The chapter closes not with another burst of creation, but with a blessing. God doesn't make anything new here. Instead, He gives away what He has made. Creation becomes co-creation; the Maker entrusts His masterpiece to those made in His image.

He entrusts it to others. This act is not just generous; it is vulnerable. The Creator steps back. The spotlight shifts.

This moment is not only a conclusion; it's a commissioning. God hands off the narrative. The humans, created in His image, are now called to act as sub-creators. They are charged with filling, tending, subduing, and stewarding the world. It is an invitation to creativity, responsibility, and relationship, with God, each other, and creation. And it is rooted in trust.

> God has hovered above the chaos;
> God has identified the boundaries;
> God has made new connections;
> God has invested in this new creation;
> God has persisted in the creative act
>   until it achieves very good;
> And now God lets the creation live.

This pattern, hovering, defining, connecting, investing, persisting, and releasing - mirrors the way God still works through us.

God blesses the image bearers, the man and the woman, and then speaks to them. He gives them their marching orders.

Be fruitful.

Multiply and fill the earth.

Subdue this new creation and all the good things that came before you. The fish. The birds. Everything that moves. All the plants and trees. And there is a plan for every beast, bird, and creeping thing: they can eat all the plants.

God had achieved what He set out to do; the creation was complete, and it was time for what's next. The man could name all the things and work the earth and start to build a family. It was complete and it was very good.

With a job well done, God then rested.

The idea of letting a creation live is both freeing and terrifying.

On one hand, it's a celebration of trust, on the other, it requires surrender. How do you know when it is time to step away? We rarely know if it is ready. What if it fails, or becomes something you never intended? Sometimes, people won't understand what you meant to say. Release is the risk love is willing to take.

Letting something live means allowing it to become something beyond your control. You are no longer tweaking and polishing and protecting. You are releasing. And sometimes the only way to understand that tension is through story.

The Writer

One of my best friends growing up was big into comics. Jeff Jensen lived a couple of blocks from me, and we went to the same school, so it was easy to spend time together. Often our time would be spent at Golden Age Collectibles, the premier Seattle comic shop tucked deep in Pike Place Market. I distinctly remember Jeff anxiously awaiting the next issues of the *Watchmen* comics when we were in high school. I'll admit it was a series that I didn't get into until much later, but Jeff was on board from the beginning.

Writer Alan Moore, artist Dave Gibbons, and colorist John Higgins used this series to deconstruct the superhero genre and hold a mirror up to the late '80s culture and politics. The series was a commercial and critical success, even being listed by Time magazine as one of the top 100 best novels published since 1923. Little did we know that the investment that Jeff put in devouring those comics would pay off many years later.

Fast forward more than 30 years and Jeff joined the writing team that brought *Watchmen* to HBO. He helped research and craft a 9-part TV series, under the direction of Damon Lindelof. It was a risk in many ways.

Lindelof and his team wanted to use *Watchmen* as an opportunity to do what the original writer did, hold a mirror up to current cultural and political issues. They aimed to tackle issues of race in America. Lindelof and Jensen, both white, have said that they walked into this process with apprehension. In interviews after the show debuted, Lindelof said he was worried that this was not necessarily their story to tell, but they went through with it anyway. A diverse team was assembled of researchers and writers who dug into the Tulsa Race Massacre of 1921 and set the show, as HBO describes it, "in an alternate history where masked vigilantes are treated as outlaws and must embrace the nostalgia, Detective Angela Abar investigates the reemergence of a white supremacist terrorist group inspired by the long-deceased moral absolutist Rorschach."

Production finished before a single viewer ever laid eyes on it. The first episode dropped in October, but unlike today's common "binge release," Watchmen came out weekly, one episode every Sunday for nine weeks. Still, to the creators, the emotional reality was the same as a binge release: the creative work was complete. Nothing could be changed. When episode one premiered, they released not just a show but their own control over it. Whatever people thought - praise, criticism, rejection - there would be no mid-course corrections, no rewrites, no opportunity to soften or redirect the message.

The response was more than anyone expected. The series captured the cultural moment. It received 26 Emmy nominations and won 11, including Outstanding Limited Series. It's now widely considered one of HBO's greatest shows. Fans keep asking for a season two, but Lindelof has said he's content to let it stand—and that if there ever is a second season, it should come from a new creative voice.

Jeff once told me that by the time the first episode aired, the team had already done the hard internal work—processing their pride, wrestling with their anxieties, facing their own hubris. They had reached a posture of humility and contentedness. Whatever came next—praise or pushback—they were prepared to receive it. When the response was overwhelmingly positive, they didn't interpret it as self-validation. Instead, Jeff said it felt like watching their creation take on a life of its own, shaped now as much by the audience's engagement as by the creators' intent.

Letting a creation live means surrendering it to others, to interpretation, to criticism, and to evolution.

It means trusting that your process, your team, and your vision were faithful, even if they aren't flawless. It is a reminder that our creations, once released, are no longer just ours. They belong to the world.

But letting something live doesn't mean it stays unchanged. Creative work has a life of its own. It grows, shifts, encounters resistance. Sometimes it drifts far from its original vision. Other times, we ourselves change, and the work no longer reflects who we are becoming. What then? What do we do when our creation is met with confusion, opposition, or unexpected transformation? This is where the next phase in the creative process begins: not the end of the story, but the beginning of a new pattern. One that requires resilience, humility, and hope.

Jeff's work on *Watchmen* reminds me that our creations, once released, no longer belong only to us. Like children, or songs, or stories, they find their own life in the world.

Just as Jeff and his team had to release their story without knowing how it would land, God, too, releases creation, knowing it will one day fall and rise again.

Order - Disorder - Reorder

There is something about creating that calls you to let go. At some point, you need to step back and allow the creation to have its place. God did this in Genesis. The world was done. It was very good. God had set the system into motion, and it was time to allow it to breathe.

What's remarkable is that it didn't have to be this way. God could have retained control, holding tightly to creation to preserve its goodness. But God didn't. God let it live.

And it unraveled almost immediately.

Genesis Chapter 3 introduces us to the fall, the moment disorder enters the ordered creation. The first humans, made in God's image and entrusted with stewardship, instead grasp for control, knowledge, and autonomy. The result is rupture: between humans and God, between humans and one another, and between humans and creation itself.

This movement from Order to Disorder is not just a moment in Genesis, it is a pattern that pulses through the entire biblical narrative. Richard Rohr, in *The Wisdom Pattern*, describes this rhythm of Order - Disorder - Reorder as the central story of transformation in Scripture, in human history, and in our individual lives. Rohr's insight isn't only theological, it's profoundly creative. Every artist, leader, or innovator must move through the same rhythm.

We see this rhythm early and often:

- In the Flood, creation is again plunged into chaos. Yet through Noah, God preserves a remnant and begins the world anew, a new order born from watery disorder.

- At Babel, human pride disrupts God's intent for shared purpose and connection. Confusion reigns. But God doesn't give up. From Abraham and Sarah, He begins a new covenant, a slow unfolding of redemption.

- In Egypt, God's people are enslaved, a profound Disorder, and God acts in dramatic fashion to bring them out. The *Exodus* is one of Scripture's great Reorderings, a deliverance that defines Israel's identity.

- But again, the people falter. The wilderness. The judges. The divided kingdoms. The exile. The silence.

- Until the Reorder that changes everything: Jesus.

Jesus is not simply a prophet or teacher, He is God Himself, stepping into His creation. In the incarnation, God does not discard the old order but enters into it, redeeming it from within. In Jesus, God inhabits the very world He formed, not to abandon it, but to redeem it and reorder it to its original intent. He takes on the weight of our brokenness, our sin, and even death itself. His crucifixion is the ultimate expression of disorder, innocence crucified, hope extinguished. But His resurrection is the definitive act of divine reordering, restoring creation, renewing life, and opening the way back to the wholeness God intended from the beginning.

This is the arc of the entire Bible. From Genesis to Revelation: Order, Disorder, Reorder.

And here's the best part: this isn't just a cosmic story. It's our story too. Every creator feels this same pattern: order, disorder, and reorder.

We are swept up into this divine rhythm. In our own lives, we mirror the same movement. We experience seasons of clarity and flourishing, times of order. Then come the interruptions: grief, doubt, failure, conflict. Disorder. And yet, by God's grace, we are never left there. God is always working to reorder, even when we cannot yet see how.

As followers of Christ, we experience this Reorder most profoundly in Baptism, where our old self is drowned and our new self rises with Christ.

Every morning, as we wake to new mercy, we participate again in the daily rhythm of dying and rising, of order undone and reordered by grace.

The Apostle Paul captures this beautifully in 2 Corinthians 5:17:

"Therefore, if anyone is in Christ, he is a new creation. The old has passed away; behold, the new has come."

Creation. Re-creation. Every day.

Rohr puts it this way: "Let go of your first order, trust the disorder, and - sometimes even hardest of all - trust the new order." We are invited not only to recognize the pattern but to participate in it. To trust that God is still creating, even in our chaos.

This isn't just a theological idea, it's a creative one. Every artist, entrepreneur, teacher, parent, or preacher knows what it is to build something with care, watch it falter, and then find a way forward. Sometimes the disorder is what opens the door to something even better.

Letting it live doesn't mean it won't change or break or be misunderstood. It means releasing it with hope, trusting that God still moves in patterns of resurrection. That very good is still possible.

That reorder is always coming.

The Choluteca Bridge

In the late 1990s, the U.S. Army Corps of Engineers built a bridge across the Choluteca River in Honduras. This wasn't just any bridge; it was engineered to endure the region's violent weather, including the hurricanes that routinely sweep across

Central America. It was considered an architectural feat.

And then Hurricane Mitch arrived in 1998. One of the deadliest storms in history, Mitch brought torrential rain and catastrophic flooding. Roads were washed away. Villages were destroyed. Rivers overflowed.

But the bridge? It stood firm. It did exactly what it was designed to do. It held.

There was just one problem. The bridge remained, but the river had moved.

The storm had reshaped the landscape. The Choluteca River, once bridged perfectly, now flowed beside it. The structure was intact, but irrelevant. It no longer served its purpose. What had been a triumph of design and durability became a bridge to nowhere.

Engineers began using it as a metaphor, but it also preaches to every creator.

Sometimes our best ideas are built for a version of reality that no longer exists.

We create with great care. We succeed. But then the world shifts. And if we aren't willing to shift with it, our creations may no longer connect.

Releasing your creation means allowing it to evolve. Letting it live means accepting that what worked beautifully yesterday might need to be adapted today. It means acknowledging that rivers move.

In creative work, whether in art, ministry, relationships, or innovation, we are called to build. But we are also called to notice when the landscape has changed.

God let the creation live, knowing full well it would shift, fall, and rise again. That wisdom invites us to do the same.

Letting Go and Living Forward

Letting your creation live can be the hardest part of the creative process. It requires trust. Trust in your work, in your collaborators, and in the world you're releasing it into. When God let creation live, it wasn't because everything was locked into perfection. It was because creation had the capacity to grow, to adapt, and to reflect God's goodness in motion.

We are invited to do the same. We shape, mold, build, invest. We reflect, revise, rework. And then, we release.

That final act is not defeat; it's discipleship.

This isn't abandonment. This is invitation. Letting it live invites new voices, new uses, and new interpretations.

Whether it's a sermon, a painting, a program, a product, or a piece of yourself you've poured into something, let it live.

Letting it live means you don't micromanage every reception or reaction. It means you don't immediately shut it down the moment things go differently than you hoped.

Letting it live means listening for what the creation is becoming, not just what it once was. It means allowing it to move from order, through disorder, into something reordered and even more resilient.

Let it live, even when the world shifts. Let it live, even if it means it needs to be rebuilt. Let it live, even if someone else carries it forward. Because once released, your creation becomes part of God's ongoing story.

Hover. Identify. Connect. Invest. Persist. Release

And then, let it live.

Because your work is not a museum piece to be guarded, it's a living story meant to grow.

Your work is alive.

It will stretch and twist and surprise you. It may fail, or flourish, or both.

But if it is faithful, if it is honest, if it is good, it will endure and evolve.

So, create well. Then let go. Let it live.

Let it grow into the next very good thing.

Because the same Spirit who hovered in the beginning still hovers, over your work, your world, and your next beginning.

Pause and Reflect

The creative life isn't linear. It loops, stretches, and surprises us. And still, the Spirit hovers: over the blank page, the broken attempt, the bold idea. Letting your work live isn't a sign of stepping away. It's an act of trust. Of making space for what comes next. The God who called creation "very good" is still creating, through you.

Questions to Consider:

What creation in your life is ready to be released?

How do you tend to respond when your plans are disrupted, or your work evolves?

Where are you currently in the rhythm of Order - Disorder - Reorder?

What do you need to let go of so that something new can live?

"The main thing is to be moved, to love, to hope, to tremble, to live."

Auguste Rodin

ORDER
DISORDER
REORDER

Order, Disorder, Reorder

The pattern of order, disorder, and reorder runs through creation itself. In Genesis, God brings order from chaos, in Genesis 3, disorder enters through sin, and through Christ, God reorders creation toward redemption. This same pattern appears throughout history's most enduring creative works.

Frankenstein

Mary Shelley first published Frankenstein when she was just 20 years old. It quickly became one of the best-known works of supernatural fiction. Thirteen years after its initial publication, the novel underwent a dramatic transformation. In the intervening years, Shelley experienced profound personal losses: two of her children and her husband, Percy, passed away, and some of her closest friends turned against her. These tragedies deeply affected her worldview, leading her to believe that free will was ineffective and that fate, or indifferent destiny, controlled events. This new perspective influenced her revision of Frankenstein. Victor Frankenstein's decision to create his creature, initially framed as a conscious choice, was recast as the result of forces beyond his control.

This revision of Frankenstein serves as a powerful example of reordering in response to personal upheaval. Shelley's creative process reflects a deep engagement with her changing understanding of humanity and destiny. The evolution of her novel invites us to consider how personal experiences can fundamentally reshape our creative work.

Mary Shelley's story mirrors the creative cycle itself; what began in the order of imagination was reshaped by the disorder of grief.

Star Wars

George Lucas's Star Wars is one of the most iconic franchises in cinematic history. The original 1977 film set box office records, redefined genres, and influenced filmmaking for decades. However, Lucas never seemed fully satisfied with his creation. More than two decades later, he began reordering the films. Using advances in digital technology, he added new backgrounds, CGI creatures, and altered key scenes (sparking debates such as "Han Shot First"). Lucas explained that these changes allowed him to bring the movies closer to his original vision.

This reordering highlights the tension between an artist's evolving vision and audience expectations. While some fans view the changes as unnecessary disruptions, others appreciate Lucas's dedication to refining his work. This example prompts us to ask: When is a creative work truly complete? And how do creators balance their vision with the audience's attachment to the original?

Lucas's endless tweaking recalls God's ongoing care for creation, not because it was imperfect, but because creativity is rarely still. Even finished work, like finished worlds, sometimes calls the creator back to refine and redeem.

The Scream

Edvard Munch's The Scream is one of the most famous works of art, depicting a figure holding its head in anguish on a pier under a blood-red sky. Often interpreted as a representation of human anxiety, what many don't realize is that Munch created multiple versions of the piece. There are two paintings, two pastels, and several prints. In 2012, one of the lesser-known pastel versions set a record as the most expensive artwork sold at auction.

Munch's iterative approach to the piece demonstrates his commitment to reordering and experimenting with the original concept. Each version offers a slightly different emotional resonance, reflecting Munch's evolving perspective. His process reminds us that revisiting a work can deepen its impact and expand its relevance.

Munch's repetitions remind us that even iteration can be revelation, each version another 'day' of creation declaring again, 'It is good.'

da Vinci

The best-known painting in the world may be the Mona Lisa. The mysterious smile painted by da Vinci has drawn people in for centuries. Recently, a French scientist, Pascal Cotte discovered that there are two other portraits under the Mona Lisa. It is believed that da Vinci worked on this painting for 14 years. Each hidden layer beneath the Mona Lisa shows an artist wrestling between what is and what could be, beauty born through patience.

Tainted Love

Few songs epitomize the 1980s like Soft Cell's Tainted Love. With its synth-pop sound and haunting melody, the 1981 hit became a cultural touchstone. What many don't know is that Tainted Love had a long history before reaching the top of the charts. Originally recorded by Gloria Jones in 1964, the song was a commercial flop. Jones tried again with a re-recording in 1973, but it saw only marginal success. It wasn't until Soft Cell reimagined it nearly two decades later that it became a global hit.

Soft Cell's version transformed the song for a new generation. Its long journey of order, disorder, and reorder shows how creativity can span decades and multiple voices, each breathing new life into the work. Sometimes, new life comes from returning to an old melody.

Walk This Way

In the mid 70s, Aerosmith was on the rise. They had a smash hit in their second album and were working on the album that would establish the band as international stars. They were also watching Mel Brooks' *Young Frankenstein*. In the film, when Dr. Frankenstein first meets Igor and invites him to 'Walk this way.' Inspiration struck and a hit song was born. The song of the same name peaked at #10 on the Billboard charts and the band continued on their successful path. By the mid 80's Aerosmith had lost a step with contemporary music. In search of a way to revitalize their career they found inspiration in the new styles that had disordered their 70's rock sensibilities. They looked back into their catalog of hits and grabbed "Walk This Way" while inviting Run DMC to join them in the studio. Not only did this reordering of their old song bring the huge success; it created a new genre of Rap/Rock music.

Songs of Surrender

If you had the chance to go back and change something in your past, would you take it? Are there things that you did or choices you made that you might like to try a different way now that you're a bit older and wiser? That's the premise behind U2's project, Songs of Surrender. Since 1976 the band has sold hundreds of millions of albums and toured non-stop. They continue to be the best band at Stadium Rock. Bono had a chance to write a book about his life. Bono and the Edge made a documentary for Disney+. In the process they discovered that life had changed, perspectives had shifted, and maybe they would do things different today if they had a chance. They revisited forty of their songs, rewriting lyrics and reimagining arrangements, a musical confession reflecting who they've become.

Their re-recordings aren't just musical, they're confessional. Like a modern psalmist, U2 revisits old songs to testify to who they've become. Reordering, for U2, isn't nostalgia; it's repentance. A creative act of owning the past while reshaping the future.

Blockbuster

Blockbuster Video was lifesaving to a kid in the '80's. At its peak, more than 80,000 employees at 9,000 stores offered copies of hit movies and classic films for a low rental fee. It seemed like we always had one or two at our house at any time. It was a perfect business model for their time, but they missed when technology moved forward. From their peak in 2004 they filed for bankruptcy in 2010. They missed the move from VHS to digital delivery. What is really crazy is that in 2000 Netflix offered to buy Blockbuster for $50 million. Blockbuster's downfall wasn't technological. It was theological. They refused to let an old form die so something new could live. Netflix did, and in doing so, it reordered an entire industry.

Netflix

Netflix began as a DVD rental service, disrupting the traditional video rental model with its mail-order system. Yet the company didn't stop there. Recognizing the potential of digital technology, Netflix transitioned to streaming video, then became a major content producer with shows like House of Cards. Through continual reordering, from mail-order DVDs to streaming to original content, Netflix redefined convenience and transformed the entertainment industry.

Each stage of Netflix's evolution involved significant risks and uncertainty. By embracing disorder and adapting to new challenges, the company not only survived but became an industry leader. This example illustrates the importance of seeing disruption as an opportunity for innovation.

Lego

Play well. That is the translation of the Danish "leg godt" – Lego. Lego started out making wooden cars and yoyos in the early 1930s. By 1949 it transitioned to plastic bricks and for decades it never looked back. By the turn of the century things started to change. The company started to see financial losses. They addressed the disorder with a reorder that diversified the toy into jewelry, clothing, and a video game. But by the mid 2000s it was looking so bleak that the CEO said "we're on a burning platform...and probably won't survive". Maybe it was the introduction of the Lego Movie, or maybe it was a commitment to simplicity and quality, but Lego made a comeback. They reordered by returning to basics: reducing brick types, trimming partnerships, and inviting fans into the creative process. Sometimes the path forward is rediscovering the simple pieces that built us.

Amazon

Back in 1994, no one had a clue what Amazon would become. Jeff Bezos was running an online bookstore from his garage. Yes, it changed the book industry, but it also changed the way we consume almost everything. Do they sell it at Target, Home Depot, Walmart? Amazon will sell it too, and bring it to your house for free, often within hours. Groceries? Sure, Amazon can do that. Maybe delivery by drone would be better? Amazon is working on that. How about creating the content we all consume? Amazon Studios is there. Amazon is constantly reordering their business and in turn reinventing the meaning of convenience. Amazon's constant reordering redefines convenience itself, an echo of the Creator's impulse to keep expanding what's possible.

Nintendo

The Nintendo brand has existed since 1889. A century before anyone would think about a computer. But Nintendo doesn't create technology they create games and tell stories. That is how they have survived. Nintendo translates as 'leave luck to heaven'. It is a testimony to their observation of disorder and drive to reorder. Nintendo has always focused on a broad consumer market. Avoiding shooter games, encouraging all ages, bringing us the GameBoy, the Wii and the Switch. There has always been a focus on fun. They have kept the business flexible, and that flexibility has allowed it to reorder with the market for nearly 150 years.

Coca-Cola

Coca-Cola's history of reordering stretches back to its beginnings in the late 19th century. Originally marketed as a cure-all for ailments, Coke evolved into one of the first global brands. Over the decades, the company adapted its image, introducing Diet Coke in the 1980s and embracing diverse marketing strategies like using Santa Claus and Olympic sponsorships.

Coca-Cola's ability to identify disorder, such as shifting consumer preferences, and respond creatively has cemented its place as a cultural icon. By returning to its core product while embracing innovation, the company demonstrates how balance between tradition and reinvention sustains longevity.

Play-Doh

Let's talk about a dramatic reorder. Play-Doh was first sold in the 30s as a cleaner to remove coal soot from wallpaper. That sells ok in the world of coal burning heat, but in the 50s the US started to move to oil and gas heat. Play-Doh was thrown into disorder. They needed some radical reordering. They heard about a schoolteacher in Cincinnati that was using their product in art class. A quick reordering of the marketing and it became a toy that has sold more than two billion cans.

Pause and Reflect

Every act of reordering is an act of faith. It means trusting that the loss of the old is not the end, but the beginning of something very good. In creativity, as in creation itself, God is always moving us from chaos to cosmos, from disorder to design, from what was to what could be.

Questions to Consider:

How has personal experience reshaped your creative endeavors, similar to Mary Shelley's evolution of Frankenstein?

What lessons can you take from George Lucas about balancing a creator's evolving vision with audience expectations?

Have you ever revisited a project like Edvard Munch's The Scream? What new insights or perspectives did you bring to it?

In your work, what disruptions or challenges could be reframed as opportunities for reordering and innovation, like Netflix or Coca-Cola?

How can reimagining past successes in new ways, like Soft Cell's Tainted Love, help you connect with a new audience or purpose?

Where in your life might God be inviting you into a season of reorder, where old forms must give way so new life can emerge?

FINAL THOUGHTS

Final Thoughts

Embracing the Genesis of Creativity

Across the pages of Genesis 1, we've seen creativity unfold in rhythm: Hovering, Identifying, Connecting, Investing, Persisting, and Releasing: a rhythm that still shapes how God creates and how we create. Each act reveals something about the creative heart of God. And about our own.

Creativity isn't reserved for the elite, or limited to fleeting moments of luck. Here's what this entire journey has taught us: creativity is woven into the very fabric of our being. The first chapter of Genesis is not just an account of how the world came to be. It is a masterclass in the creative process. It teaches us that creativity is divine, that it thrives within boundaries, requires patience and risk, invites investment, and ultimately calls for trust.

But more than that, it teaches us this: you were made to create.

From the very beginning, God has revealed Himself as Creator. The Father speaks, the Son is the Word through whom all things are made, and the Spirit hovers, present, active, and preparing. That same triune God has made you in His image, placing His creative imprint on your very being.

We began this journey with God's Spirit hovering over the waters; we end with that same Spirit hovering over the possibilities within you.

You Were Made to Create

God's first recorded act was not judgment, war, or even worship. It was creation. He shaped a world with order and beauty, form and fullness. And He called it good.

If this is how God first revealed Himself, what might that say about how we were meant to live?

And here's the invitation, you reflect that same divine impulse every time you bring something new into the world. Whether it's a painting or a business, a classroom lesson or a restored relationship, a solution to a thorny problem or a Saturday night meal plan scribbled on a napkin.

Creativity is not limited to studios and stages. It's not about fame or perfection. It's about faithful participation in the creative rhythm of God.

The Rhythms of Creativity

The Genesis account shows us how to live creatively:

- Hover over the chaos, don't flinch. Take it in.

- Identify the boundaries, don't resent them. Embrace the clarity they provide.

- Connect what belongs together, between ideas, people, disciplines, and past and future.

- Invest yourself fully, creativity without cost rarely transforms.

- Persist until it becomes very good, not perfect, but deeply, truly good.

- Release it, let it live, allow your work into the world with faith.

These aren't just steps.

They're a lifestyle.

A vocation.

A calling.

What Now?

So, what will you create?

What is hovering just beneath the surface, waiting to be spoken into light? What ideas are brooding in the deep, waiting for someone to name them, shape them, bless them, and call them good?

Maybe, you're standing at the edge of something new.

Maybe, you're in the messy middle.

Maybe, your creative voice has been silent for too long.

The courage to create is not the absence of fear. It is the willingness to begin anyway.

You don't go alone, because the same Spirit who hovered over the deep now hovers over your life. Ready to bring light, order, and renewal.

And that's where we end this part of the journey.

Because the story of creation didn't stop in Genesis 1; the Spirit still hovers.

> *"The earth was without form and void, and darkness was over the face of the deep. And the Spirit of God was hovering over the face of the waters."*
>
> **Genesis 1:2**

Before there was light, before land and sky, before there was time as we know it, the Spirit hovered.

In Exodus, the Spirit filled artisans with skill and wisdom to build a dwelling where heaven could meet earth. At Pentecost, the same Spirit filled ordinary people, transforming them into extraordinary witnesses.

From creation to tabernacle to church, the Spirit's creativity has always been about making space for God to dwell among us.

The Spirit hovered then, and hovers still.

The Spirit hovers over your chaos too,

Over the blank page,

Over the broken plan,

Over the job you're not sure you're qualified for,

Over the idea you've been afraid to share,

Over the family you're trying to hold together,

Over the creation you've begun but not yet finished,

Over the life that's still unfolding.

The Father creates,

The Son redeems,

The Spirit still hovers.

You are not alone in your creating. You were never meant to be.

So hover. Observe. Embrace the constraints. Invest your heart. Be patient. Push for "very good."

And when it's time, let it live.

**Because the God who creates,
does not abandon what He begins.**

He sustains it.

He fills it.

He redeems it.

And through you, He keeps creating.

You were made to speak light into darkness, to separate and shape, to see and bless.

Not for perfection. Not for applause.

But as an image-bearer of a God who hovers, shapes, blesses, and releases.

Every act of creativity begins again with a new Genesis, a moment when light pierces the dark and something unseen starts to take form.

What will you make with what you've been given?

This is not just the end of a book, it's the beginning of your Genesis.

Pause and Reflect

Questions to Consider:

What is one small act of creativity you feel called to begin, or begin again?

Where do you sense the Spirit hovering in your life right now?

What fears or doubts do you need to release in order to let your work live?

How can your creativity join God's ongoing work of renewal and hope in the world?

The Genesis of this Book

Creativity doesn't emerge in a vacuum. Just as God hovered over the chaos, observed, connected, and invested in creation, I have hovered over the work of others, marinating in their stories, insights, and breakthroughs. The books, films, songs, podcasts, and artworks listed below were not only influential in shaping this book but also helped shape me. They gave me language for the journey, courage to stay in the work, and a broader perspective on what creativity means. This is by no means a comprehensive list, but I share them here with gratitude and with the hope that they might inspire your creative path as well.

Books That Inspired The Genesis of Creativity

Creative Process & Innovation

Books that explore how creativity is formed, sustained, and unlocked across disciplines.

Steal Like an Artist – Austin Kleon
On remixing inspiration and embracing authenticity.

The Creative Habit – Twyla Tharp
    A practical guide to disciplined creative living.

Creativity Sucks – Phil Hansen
    On creative limits as springboards.

How to Think Like Leonardo da Vinci – Michael Gelb
    Practices for genius-level thinking.

Flying, Falling, Catching – Henri Nouwen
    On trust, surrender, and the creative freefall of faith.

Tell It Slant – Eugene Peterson
    A poetic take on language, scripture, and truth-telling.

Spark – Claudia Kalb
    A study of the origin of genius.

Flatland – Edwin Abbott
    A satirical lens on dimensional thinking.

Originals – Adam Grant
    How nonconformists fuel change.

Contagious – Jonah Berger
    What makes ideas and content spread.

Moonwalking with Einstein – Joshua Foer
    On memory, observation, and mental curation.

The Wisdom Pattern – Richard Rohr
    On the spiritual rhythm of order, disorder, and reorder.

The Art of Racing in the Rain – Garth Stein
Storytelling from a deeply unique perspective.

The Birth of Loud – Ian S. Port
On the rivalry that shaped modern music.

The Wrecking Crew – Kent Hartman
The secret creative force behind decades of music.

Salt – Mark Kurlansky
A history of one element's impact on the world.

Mosquito – Timothy C. Winegard
How a tiny creature shaped human history.

Faith, Theology & Scripture

Books that examine biblical engagement, Christian theology, and the spiritual imagination.

The Brothers Karamazov – Fyodor Dostoevsky
A profound dive into faith, doubt, and meaning.

Inspired – Rachel Held Evans
Wrestling with Scripture and embracing divine mystery.

What If Jesus Was Serious? – Skye Jethani
Playful yet profound reframing of faith and wisdom.

Faith That Engages the Culture – Costanzo & Packiam
   Theology that listens and leads.

Boundaries – Cloud & Townsend
   On setting healthy limits in life and work.

Centered-Set Church – Mark D. Baker
   Rethinking how we define inclusion and community.

Wittenberg vs. Geneva – Brian W. Thomas
   Exploring theological identity.

Lutheran Questions, Lutheran Answers – Martin E. Marty
   Straightforward responses to complex doctrines.

Welcoming But Not Affirming – Stanley J. Grenz
   A theological perspective on inclusion and ethics.

Misreading Scripture with Western Eyes – Richards & O'Brien
   Exposing cultural blind spots in biblical interpretation.

God and Churchill – Sandys & Henley
   Divine purpose in history and leadership.

Brand Luther – Andrew Pettegree
   How Martin Luther rebranded the Church through media.

The State of Religion & Young People 2022 – Springtide Research Institute
   Gen Z's spiritual and mental health needs.

Writing, Storytelling & Communication

Memoirs, techniques, and reflections on how language and story shape the world.

On Writing – Stephen King
    Half memoir, half writing masterclass.

Bossypants – Tina Fey
    Comedy, chaos, and creative leadership.

Born Standing Up – Steve Martin
    A memoir of comedy, timing, and grit.

I Must Say – Martin Short
    A comic's journey of loss and joy.

Building a StoryBrand – Donald Miller
    A communication strategy rooted in clarity and narrative.

Blue Like Jazz – Donald Miller
    A spiritual memoir of messy grace.

If I Only Knew Then – Charles Grodin
    Reflections from a lifetime of performance and regret.

A Prayer for Owen Meany – John Irving
    A masterclass in narrative voice and destiny.

The Catcher in the Rye – J.D. Salinger
    A literary act of cultural disruption.

Our Gang – Terry Lee
A satirical look at politics, power, and identity.

Leadership, Teams & Organizational Culture

Wisdom from business, sports, and organizational development that informs healthy leadership.

The Five Dysfunctions of a Team – Patrick Lencioni
On overcoming collaboration barriers.

Working Together – Michael Eisner
Creative partnerships from Disney's inner circle.

Leading Change – John Kotter
Essential strategies for transformation.

Decisive – Chip & Dan Heath
How to make better decisions.

Eleven Rings – Phil Jackson
Leadership lessons from a Zen-influenced coach.

Miracles on the Hardwood – Dan Wetzel
Faith, basketball, and community.

Dream Team – Jack McCallum
The ultimate story of collaboration and legacy.

Branding, Marketing & Strategy

Books that uncover the mechanics of influence, messaging, and cultural impact.

Branding Faith – Phil Cooke
   Sharing eternal truth in modern contexts.

Building Strong Brands – David Aaker
   Foundational frameworks for brand identity.

This Is Marketing – Seth Godin
   Reaching people through resonance.

All Marketers Are Liars – Seth Godin
   How authentic storytelling builds trust.

The 22 Immutable Laws of Marketing – Ries & Trout
   Strategy essentials for the attention economy.

Positioning – Ries & Trout
   On carving out a distinct identity in a noisy marketplace.

Cultural Insight, Psychology & Sociology

Books that explore how people think, how culture shapes us, and how systems evolve.

Think Again – Adam Grant
    A toolkit for cognitive flexibility.

Them – Ben Sasse
    A commentary on division and community.

Skin in the Game – Nassim Nicholas Taleb
    Why real risk matters in creative work.

The Silo Effect – Gillian Tett
    How breaking down organizational walls fuels creativity.

Talking to Strangers – Malcolm Gladwell
    On miscommunication and modern trust.

David and Goliath – Malcolm Gladwell
    Underdogs, misfits, and the art of battling giants.

Outliers – Malcolm Gladwell
    What makes high-achievers different.

Blink – Malcolm Gladwell
    The power of thinking without thinking.

Biographies & Personal Journeys

Profiles in perseverance, transformation, and creative risk across a variety of fields.

Shoe Dog – Phil Knight
    The gripping founding story of Nike.

Elon Musk – Ashlee Vance
    A portrait of ambition and disruption.

Van Gogh: The Life – Steven Naifeh
    A masterwork on a troubled genius.

Michelangelo – Miles Unger
    Divine and human tension in art.

Unbroken – Laura Hillenbrand
    Survival, resilience, and purpose in war.

The Great Bridge – David McCullough
    Engineering brilliance and creative endurance.

Films & TV Shows That Inspired The Genesis of Creativity

Watchmen (HBO)
    A reimagining of myth and justice in the creative act of letting go.

Dead Poets Society
    On creativity, mentorship, and living deliberately.

The Matrix
    A bold metaphor for waking up to new realities.

Pixar films (especially *Toy Story*)
    On creating within technological boundaries and learning through iteration.

Frankenstein (various adaptations)
    On persistence, revision, and the unintended consequences of creative ambition.

Lost
A serialized epic about mystery, interconnectedness, leadership, and narrative risk-taking.

Pushing Daisies
Vibrant visual storytelling with tight narrative rules; whimsical yet emotionally grounded.

The Dick Van Dyke Show
A celebration of creative work-life balance; pioneering comedy inside network constraints.

Twin Peaks
Experimental narrative wrapped in small-town surrealism; disorder and mystery as creative space.

Community
A wild collage of influences where each homage, parody, and meta twist becomes raw material for something unexpectedly original.

Psych
A playful masterclass in seeing what others miss, proving that creativity begins with paying closer attention.

The Twilight Zone (original)
Compact storytelling that defies genre and time; creative constraint at its peak.

The Good Place
Whimsical theology and ethical inquiry housed in sharp writing and inventive world-building.

Ted Lasso
A case study in emotional intelligence, vulnerability, and long-game creative investment.

Severance
    A haunting metaphor for creative and spiritual fragmentation, and the cost of compartmentalized living.

Inside Out
    Pixar's exploration of emotional boundaries and integration through rich, constrained storytelling.

Everything Everywhere All At Once
    A maximalist meditation on chaos, meaning, creativity, and radical acceptance.

Whiplash
    The brutal pursuit of greatness, where boundaries are broken and rebuilt.

Amadeus
    A reflection on envy, divine inspiration, and artistic legacy.

Podcasts & Interviews That Inspired The Genesis of Creativity

Fresh Air with Steve Martin
    On the tireless crafting behind seemingly effortless comedy.

Celtics Radio with Kyrie Irving
    A rare glimpse into creative goals, discipline, and fatherly influence.

Oprah Winfrey (*Super Soul Conversations*)
    Reflections on progress over perfection, presence, and inner growth.

Bono (Songs of Surrender interviews)
    Meditations on songwriting, vulnerability, and faith in disorder.

Stuff You Should Know
    Curiosity meets clarity; hovering over strange topics and revealing unexpected connections.

The Ezra Klein Show
    Deep-dive conversations across disciplines; creativity as sustained inquiry.

On Being with Krista Tippett
    Poetry, theology, and wisdom intersect, hovering over the mystery of human experience.

Song Exploder
    Musicians take apart one song and tell the story of its creation, boundaries, revisions, and breakthroughs.

Hidden Brain
    A look into the psychology behind behavior and decision-making, how creativity is often unconscious and shaped by unseen forces.

Revisionist History (Malcolm Gladwell)
    Retelling the overlooked, the misunderstood, the misfiled, creative reframing in action.

Design Matters with Debbie Millman
    Candid interviews with designers and artists on the emotional roots of creative work.

Armchair Expert (with Dax Shepard)
    Playful yet serious interviews that reveal how failure, recovery, and self-awareness shape creativity.

Art & Architecture That Inspired The Genesis of Creativity

Dale Chihuly – *Basket* and *Macchia* series
On making surprising connections through repetition, transparency, and organic chaos.

Frank Gehry – Disney Concert Hall, Guggenheim Bilbao, MoPop
On reshaping what architecture can be by embracing constraints and dissonance.

Edvard Munch – *The Scream* (multiple versions)
On evolving emotion and meaning over time; expression as disorder and release.

Michelangelo – *The Last Judgment*, Sistine Chapel Ceiling
On embedding yourself in your creation, literally painting your own likeness into the act of judgment.

The Parthenon – Athens
Order, proportion, and enduring beauty in stone. A masterpiece of constraint and intentionality, each column slightly curved to correct optical illusion. Creativity built on unseen adjustments.

St. Peter's Basilica – Vatican
Lavish, awe-inspiring, and spiritually charged. The scale reminds us of how creativity can embody faith, while also provoking questions about humility, excess, and legacy.

Music That Inspired The Genesis of Creativity

The Beatles – Hamburg years & early albums
On observation, repetition, and immersion. The

creative engine wasn't sudden genius, it was
playing 8 hours a night, absorbing everything, and r
reshaping it in community.

Queen – *Bohemian Rhapsody*
A masterclass in slow-cooked brilliance, multi-genre integration, and unflinching originality. Creativity that refused to fit the mold.

U2 – *Songs of Surrender*
A spiritual revisiting of past work; reordering what was once defiant into something contemplative. Proof that creativity matures alongside the artist.

Soft Cell – *Tainted Love*
A creative reimagining of a B-side soul song that became an '80s icon. On the power of taking overlooked raw material and seeing something new.

Aerosmith & Run-DMC – *Walk This Way*
On genre-busting collaboration. Two worlds meet - rock and rap - and something entirely new is born. Creativity thrives at intersections.

NOTES

Introduction

Genesis 1:1–31. *The Holy Bible*, English Standard Version. Wheaton, IL: Crossway, 2016.

Cloud, Henry, and John Townsend. *Boundaries: When to Say Yes, How to Say No to Take Control of Your Life*. Updated and Expanded ed. Grand Rapids, MI: Zondervan, 2017.

Lucasfilm Ltd. *Star Wars: Episode IV – A New Hope*. Directed by George Lucas. 20th Century Fox, 1977.

Middleton, J. Richard. *The Liberating Image: The Imago Dei in Genesis 1*. Grand Rapids, MI: Brazos Press, 2005.

Bauckham, Richard. *The Bible and Ecology: Rediscovering the Community of Creation*. Waco, TX: Baylor University Press, 2010.

Robinson, Ken. *Out of Our Minds: Learning to Be Creative*. Oxford: Capstone, 2001.

Chapter 1

The Holy Bible, English Standard Version. Wheaton, IL: Crossway, 2016. Genesis 1:1–31; 1:26; Exodus 31:1–11; Psalm 19:1; Psalm 46:10; Matthew 6:28–29.

Berra, Yogi. *The Yogi Book: "I Really Didn't Say Everything I Said!"* New York: Workman Publishing, 1998.

Bauckham, Richard. *The Bible and Ecology: Rediscovering the Community of Creation*. Waco, TX: Baylor University Press, 2010.

Kelley, Tom, and David Kelley. *Creative Confidence: Unleashing the Creative Potential Within Us All*. New York: Crown Business, 2013.

Walton, John H. *The Lost World of the Israelite Conquest*. Downers Grove, IL: IVP Academic, 2017.

O'Connor, Flannery. "Writing and Faith." In *Mystery and Manners: Occasional Prose*, edited by Sally and Robert Fitzgerald, 233–242. New York: Farrar, Straus and Giroux, 1969.

Brueggemann, Walter. *Sabbath as Resistance: Saying No to the Culture of Now*. Louisville, KY: Westminster John Knox Press, 2014.

Chapter 2

Angelou, Maya. "Everybody born comes from the Creator trailing wisps of glory…" Quoted in *Conversations with Maya Angelou*, edited by Jeffrey M. Elliot. Jackson: University Press of Mississippi, 1989.

de Bono, Edward. "There is no doubt that creativity is the most important human resource…" In *Serious Creativity: Using the Power of Lateral Thinking to Create New Ideas*. New York: HarperBusiness, 1992.

The Holy Bible, English Standard Version. Wheaton, IL: Crossway, 2016. (Genesis 4 references to Jabal, Jubal, Tubal-Cain)

TED.com. "Talks on Creativity." Accessed July 10, 2025. https://www.ted.com/topics/creativity

Pallotta, Dan. *"The Real Problem with Charity."* TED Talk, March 2013. https://www.ted.com/talks/dan_pallotta_the_way_we_think_about_charity_is_dead_wrong

IBM. *Capitalizing on Complexity: Insights from the Global Chief Executive Officer Study.* IBM Global Business Services, 2010.

Yale Center for Emotional Intelligence. *"Emotion and Creativity in the Workplace."* Accessed July 10, 2025. https://ei.yale.edu

McKinsey & Company. *"Diversity Wins: How Inclusion Matters."* May 2020. https://www.mckinsey.com

Schmidt, Eric, and Jonathan Rosenberg. *How Google Works.* New York: Grand Central Publishing, 2014. (For Google's "20% Time" policy)

Kim, Kyung Hee. *"The Creativity Crisis: The Decrease in Creative Thinking Scores on the Torrance Tests of Creative Thinking."* Creativity Research Journal 23, no. 4 (2011): 285–295.

Adobe. *Creativity and Education: Why it Matters. Adobe Education Study*, 2013. https://www.adobe.com/education/pdf/adobe-creativity-and-education-thought-leadership-paper.pdf

Concordia University Irvine. *"Enduring Questions & Ideas (Q&I) Core Curriculum."* Accessed July 10, 2025. https://www.cui.edu/academicprograms/undergraduate/general-education/qi-core

Myers, Makenna. Quoted in *"Enduring Questions & Ideas (Q&I) Core Curriculum."* Concordia University Irvine. Accessed July 10, 2025.

National Geographic. *"10 Inventions That Changed the World."* Accessed July 10, 2025. https://www.nationalgeographic.com

Pink, Daniel H. *A Whole New Mind: Why Right-Brainers Will Rule the Future*. New York: Riverhead Books, 2005.

Brown, Tim. *Change by Design: How Design Thinking Creates New Alternatives for Business and Society*. Boston: Harvard Business Press, 2009.

Lorne Michaels. "To me there's no creativity without boundaries…" Quoted in: Shales, Tom, and James Andrew Miller. *Live From New York: The Complete Uncensored History of Saturday Night Live*. Boston: Little, Brown and Company, 2002.

Chapter 3

Einstein, Albert. *The Ultimate Quotable Einstein*, edited by Alice Calaprice. Princeton: Princeton University Press, 2010.

The Holy Bible, English Standard Version. Wheaton, IL: Crossway, 2016.

The Message: The Bible in Contemporary Language, trans. Eugene H. Peterson. Colorado Springs, CO: NavPress, 2002.

Gladwell, Malcolm. *Outliers: The Story of Success*. New York: Little, Brown and Company, 2008.

Spitz, Bob. *The Beatles: The Biography*. New York: Little, Brown and Company, 2005.

Abbott, Edwin A. *Flatland: A Romance of Many Dimensions*. London: Seeley & Co., 1884.

Doyle, Arthur Conan. "A Scandal in Bohemia." In *The Adventures of Sherlock Holmes*. London: George Newnes, 1892.

Eikenberry, Kevin. *"Six Ways to Improve Your Powers of Observation."* KevinEikenberry.com. Accessed July 10, 2025. https://blog.kevineikenberry.com/leadership-supervisory-skills/6-ways-to-improve-your-powers-of-observation.

Foer, Joshua. *Moonwalking with Einstein: The Art and Science of Remembering Everything*. New York: Penguin Press, 2011.

McCullough, David. Interview by NEH. *"The Human Spirit."* National Endowment for the Humanities, September 2005. https://www.neh.gov/humanities/2005/september-october/conversation/conversation-david-mccullough.

Lotz, Anne Graham. *"Billy Graham's Daughter: He Was His Message."* Christianity Today, February 21, 2018. https://www.christianitytoday.com/news/2018/february/billy-graham-daughter-he-was-his-message-anne-lotz.html.

Disney, Walt. Quoted in *Meet the Robinsons*, directed by Stephen J. Anderson. Walt Disney Pictures, 2007.

Berra, Yogi. Widely attributed quote: "You can observe a lot just by watching."

The Beatles (Complete Playlist). Spotify. Accessed July 10, 2025.

Lewisohn, Mark. *Tune In: The Beatles: All These Years, Volume* 1. New York: Crown Archetype, 2013.

Chapter 4

The Holy Bible, English Standard Version. Wheaton, IL: Crossway, 2016. (Genesis 1:3–5)

Cloud, Henry and Townsend, John. *Boundaries: When to Say Yes, How to Say No to Take Control of Your Life*. With John Townsend. Grand Rapids, MI: Zondervan, 1992.

Gehry, Frank. Quotes and context drawn from public interviews and architectural commentary; for comprehensive coverage, see: Goldberger, Paul. B*uilding Art: The Life and Work of Frank Gehry*. New York: Knopf, 2015.

Yun, J. *"Architectural Creativity and the Transformation of Construction."* Journal of Urban Architecture, 2003. (You may need to substitute with an alternate academic source if this citation was created for illustrative purposes.)

Stravinsky, Igor. *Poetics of Music in the Form of Six Lessons*. Cambridge, MA: Harvard University Press, 1970.

Tlingit Myth. *"Raven Steals the Light."* World Mythology, CCCOnline Pressbooks, 2020.

Plato. *The Republic*. Translated by Desmond Lee. London: Penguin Classics, 1969. (paraphrase)

Boyd, Ryan. *"Creativity Inside the Box: Revisiting Guilford's Nine-Dot Puzzle."* Creativity Research Journal, 2014.

Fredine, Patrick. *"Breaking the Box: Why Creativity Requires Constraints."* Business Innovation Quarterly, 2018.

Furtick, Steven. *Sun Stand Still: What Happens When You Dare to Ask God for the Impossible*. Colorado Springs: Multnomah Books, 2011.

Groeschel, Craig. *Divine Direction: 7 Decisions That Will Change Your Life*. Grand Rapids: Zondervan, 2017.

Chopra, Deepak. *Reinventing the Body, Resurrecting the Soul.* New York: Harmony Books, 2009.

Jakes, T. D. *Instinct: The Power to Unleash Your Inborn Drive.* New York: FaithWords, 2014.

Gladwell, Malcolm. Quoted in various interviews; see also *What the Dog Saw.* New York: Little, Brown and Company, 2009.

Banksy. "Think outside the box, collapse the box..." Quoted in *Wall and Piece.* London: Century, 2005.

Pixar. Referenced via "20% Time" innovation model and Toy Story development challenges. See: Catmull, Ed. *Creativity, Inc.* New York: Random House, 2014.

Edison, Thomas. Quote about iterative experiments widely attributed. See: Baldwin, Neil. *Edison: Inventing the Century.* New York: Hyperion, 2001.

Ennaceur, Amed, and Jocelyne Delacour. "A New One-Trial Test for Neurobiological Studies of Memory in Rats." Behavioural Brain Research 31, no. 1 (1988): 47–59.

Maya, Susan. "*Fences and Freedom: How Boundaries Encourage Creative Play.*" Journal of Childhood Development, 2018.

Casper, Monique. "*Creativity and Culture in Higher Education.*" Journal of Educational Practice, 2013.

Davis, Lee N. "*Spanning the Creative Space Between Home and Work: Leisure Time, Hobbies and Organizational Creativity.*" DRUID Conference, Copenhagen, June 2013.

237

Al-Eraky, Mohamed M., and Hesham F. Marei. "Patterns, Trends and Thinking 'Inside' the Box in Medical Education." Medical Education 49, no. 12 (2015): 1176–1186.

Dahl, Darren W., and Page Moreau. "The Influence and Value of Analogical Thinking During New Product Ideation." Journal of Marketing Research 44, no. 4 (2007): 500–510.

Kohrman, David. "While My Guitar Gently Weeps: The Story Behind the Song." Rolling Stone Archives, 2014.

Stokes, Patricia D. "Crossing Disciplines: A Constraint-Based Model of the Creative Process." Journal of Product Innovation Management 30, Supplement 1 (2014): E4–E18.

Baer, John. "Domain Specificity and the Limits of Creativity Theory." Journal of Creative Behavior 46, no. 1 (2012): 16–29.

Winfrey, Danielle. "The 500 Most Creative People Alive." Red Bull Media House, 2016. https://www.redbull.com/int-en/projects/500-most-creative-people-report.

Michaels, Lorne. Quoted in multiple interviews; see: Shales, Tom, and James Andrew Miller. Live from New York: An Uncensored History of Saturday Night Live. Boston: Little, Brown and Company, 2002.

Chapter 5

The Holy Bible, English Standard Version. Wheaton, IL: Crossway, 2016. (Genesis 1:26, 31; Exodus 31:2–3; Acts 2:42, 44)

Isaacson, Walter. Steve Jobs. New York: Simon & Schuster, 2011.

Kahn, Robert. Quoted in various commentaries on shalom and Jewish ethics. See, for example, *Echoes of the Soul: A Rabbi's Reflections on Life.*

Chihuly: On Color and Form. Seattle: Portland Press, 2010.

Chihuly Garden and Glass. Accessed July 10, 2025. https://www.chihulygardenandglass.com

Thoreau, Henry David. *Walden.* Boston: Ticknor and Fields, 1854.

Calaprice, Alice, ed. *The Ultimate Quotable Einstein.* Princeton: Princeton University Press, 2010.

Baldwin, Neil. Edison: *Inventing the Century.* New York: Hyperion, 2001.

Naifeh, Steven, and Gregory White Smith. *Van Gogh: The Life.* New York: Random House, 2011.

Roskill, Mark, ed. *The Letters of Vincent van Gogh.* New York: Touchstone, 1997.

Kleon, Austin. *Steal Like an Artist: 10 Things Nobody Told You About Being Creative.* New York: Workman Publishing, 2012.

"Jim Jarmusch's 5 Golden Rules of Filmmaking." MovieMaker Magazine, Spring 2004.

Chapter 6

The Holy Bible, English Standard Version. Wheaton, IL: Crossway, 2016. (Genesis 1:26–27, Ephesians 2:10)

Ellington, Duke. Quoted in: Teachout, Terry. *Duke: A Life of Duke Ellington.* New York: Gotham Books, 2013.

McKnight, Scot. *The Blue Parakeet: Rethinking How You Read the Bible.* Grand Rapids, MI: Zondervan, 2008.

Baldwin, Neil. *Edison: Inventing the Century.* New York: Hyperion, 2001.

Calaprice, Alice, ed. *The Ultimate Quotable Einstein.* Princeton: Princeton University Press, 2010.

Naifeh, Steven, and Gregory White Smith. *Van Gogh: The Life.* New York: Random House, 2011.

Roskill, Mark, ed. *The Letters of Vincent van Gogh.* New York: Touchstone, 1997.

Tesh, John. *Relentless: Unleashing a Life of Purpose, Grit, and Faith.* Nashville: Thomas Nelson, 2020.

MoMA. *The Artist Is Present.* Museum of Modern Art Exhibition, March–May 2010. https://www.moma.org/calendar/exhibitions/964

Abramović, Marina. *Walk Through Walls: A Memoir.* New York: Crown Archetype, 2016.

Clark, Kenneth. *Civilisation: A Personal View.* London: BBC Books, 1969.

Biskind, Peter. *Easy Riders, Raging Bulls: How the Sex-Drugs-and-Rock 'n' Roll Generation Saved Hollywood.* New York: Simon & Schuster, 1998.

Kleon, Austin. *Steal Like an Artist: 10 Things Nobody Told You About Being Creative.* New York: Workman Publishing, 2012.

Twain, Mark. *The Innocents Abroad*. Hartford: American Publishing Company, 1869.

Chapter 7

The Holy Bible, English Standard Version. Wheaton, IL: Crossway, 2016. (Genesis 1:26–31; Genesis 2:2)

Van Gogh, Vincent. Quoted in: Roskill, Mark, ed. *The Letters of Vincent van Gogh*. New York: Touchstone, 1997.

Prince. *The Beautiful Ones*. New York: Spiegel & Grau, 2019.

Dalí, Salvador. Widely attributed quote. See: Descharnes, Robert. Salvador *Dalí: The Paintings*. Cologne: Taschen, 2007.

Winfrey, Oprah. Quoted in: *O, The Oprah Magazine*, January 2009.

Rowling, J.K. *Very Good Lives: The Fringe Benefits of Failure and the Importance of Imagination*. New York: Little, Brown and Company, 2015.

Mercury, Freddie. "Bohemian Rhapsody." In: Queen. *A Night at the Opera*. EMI Records, 1975. See also: Blake, Mark. *Is This the Real Life? The Untold Story of Queen*. Cambridge: Da Capo Press, 2011.

Canemaker, John. *Walt Disney's Nine Old Men and the Art of Animation*. New York: Disney Editions, 2001.

Crichton, Michael. *Jurassic Park*. New York: Alfred A. Knopf, 1990.

Martin, Steve. Interview by Terry Gross. *Fresh Air*, NPR, March 2008. https://www.npr.org/templates/story/story.php?storyId=88415030

Martin, Steve. *Born Standing Up: A Comic's Life*. New York: Scribner, 2007.

Fey, Tina. *Bossypants*. New York: Reagan Arthur Books, 2011.

Seinfeld, *Jerry. Is This Anything?* New York: Simon & Schuster, 2020.

Chapter 8

The Holy Bible, English Standard Version. Wheaton, IL: Crossway, 2016. (Genesis 1:28–31; Genesis 2:2; Genesis 3; 2 Corinthians 5:17)

Rohr, Richard. *The Wisdom Pattern: Order, Disorder, Reorder*. Cincinnati: Franciscan Media, 2020.

Watchmen. Created by Damon Lindelof. HBO, 2019. Based on the graphic novel by Alan Moore, Dave Gibbons, and John Higgins.

Time Magazine. "All-TIME 100 Novels." Time.com. Accessed July 10, 2025. https://time.com/collection/100-best-books/

The Verge. *"Damon Lindelof on Ending Watchmen: It's Time to Let It Be."* Interview by Andrew Liptak. January 2020. https://www.theverge.com/2020/1/22/watchmen-hbo-finale-damon-lindelof-interview

U.S. Army Corps of Engineers. *"Choluteca Bridge Case Study."* Engineering Resilience Archive, 1999.

National Geographic. *"Hurricane Mitch: Devastation in Central America."* Published November 1998. https://www.nationalgeographic.com/environment/article/hurricane-mitch

The Atlantic. *"The Bridge That Went Nowhere."* Commentary on Choluteca Bridge as metaphor. Accessed July 10, 2025.

Chapter 9

Rohr, Richard. *The Wisdom Pattern: Order, Disorder, Reorder.* Cincinnati: Franciscan Media, 2020.Shelley, Mary. Frankenstein; or, The Modern Prometheus. 1818. Revised edition, 1831.

Lucas, George. *Star Wars: A New Hope.* Directed by George Lucas. Lucasfilm Ltd., 1977.

Young Frankenstein. Directed by Mel Brooks. 20th Century Fox, 1974.

"Han Shot First." Wookieepedia. Accessed July 10, 2025. https://starwars.fandom.com/wiki/Han_shot_first.

Munch, Edvard. *The Scream.* Multiple versions, 1893–1910.

Vogel, Carol. *"A Pastel Version of Edvard Munch's 'The Scream' Brings $120 Million at Sotheby's."* The New York Times, May 2, 2012.

Cotte, Pascal. *"Secrets of the Mona Lisa Revealed."* Lumiere Technology, 2015.

Soft Cell. *"Tainted Love."* Non-Stop Erotic Cabaret, Some Bizzare Records, 1981.

Jones, Gloria. *"Tainted Love."* Champion Records, 1964.

Aerosmith and Run DMC. *"Walk This Way."* Def Jam/Geffen Records, 1986.

U2. *Songs of Surrender*. Island Records, 2023.

Bono & The Edge: A Sort of Homecoming with Dave Letterman. Disney+, 2023.

"Blockbuster Video." Encyclopedia Britannica. Accessed July 10, 2025. https://www.britannica.com/topic/Blockbuster-LLC.

Netflix. "A Brief History." Netflix Media Center. Accessed July 10, 2025. https://about.netflix.com/en.

Lego. "History Timeline." Lego Group. Accessed July 10, 2025. https://www.lego.com/en-us/aboutus/lego-group/the-lego-history.

Bezos, Jeff. "Amazon's First Letter to Shareholders." Amazon, 1997.

Nintendo. "Company History." Nintendo Official Site. Accessed July 10, 2025. https://www.nintendo.com/corp/history.

Allen, Frederick. *Secret Formula: How Brilliant Marketing and Relentless Salesmanship Made Coca-Cola the Best-Known Product in the World*. HarperBusiness, 1994.

Milestones in Coca-Cola History. The Coca-Cola Company. Accessed July 10, 2025. https://www.coca-colacompany.com.

Play-Doh. "History of Play-Doh." Hasbro Official Site. Accessed July 10, 2025. https://corporate.hasbro.com/en-us/playdoh-history.

Chapter 10

Genesis 1:1–31, English Standard Version.

Genesis 1:2, English Standard Version.

Exodus 31:1–5, English Standard Version.

Acts 2:1–4, English Standard Version.

Genesis 1:28, English Standard Version.

Genesis 1:31, English Standard Version.

THANK YOU!

To my wife, my kids, and my grandkids I see the creativity in each
of you every day, even if you miss it sometimes.

To my parents and grandparents, who opened the door for me
to step into a creative life rooted in faith and imagination.

To Diane, who slogged her way through the first draft
and helped me see the potential of what this could be.

To Erik, who lent an artist's eye to layout and design,
bringing visual life to the words on these pages.

To Jenn, who spotted the deep cuts that brought clarity and
unity to the story this book was trying to tell.

To Tanner, who guided me down a path he's traveled before,
offering wisdom born of experience.

To Dan, who brought a pastoral backstop to the theology of it
all, grounding creative insight in faithful truth.

To the friends, mentors, and colleagues who encouraged,
challenged, and inspired me along the way.

And to every reader willing to explore these pages
may you discover the creativity that has been in you all along.

ABOUT BIL HOOD

Bil Hood is a creative leader, pastor, author, and veteran event producer whose work blends faith, storytelling, and innovation. Over his career, he has produced large-scale experiences for brands like Microsoft, Disney, Intel, and Nintendo, as well as faith-based organizations and schools across the western U.S. At Concordia University Irvine, he has led initiatives including 1,000 person service projects, the award-winning Reformation 500 celebration at Segerstrom Concert Hall, and nationally broadcast PBS Christmas specials.

Creativity has been a lifelong throughline, from leading bands and recording award-winning music to crafting messages that inspire action. Ordained through Concordia Seminary, he brings both theological depth and practical leadership to every project. He holds a Master's in Organizational Leadership and has a track record of connecting ideas, people, and possibilities to create meaningful impact.

Bil lives in Southern California with his wife, Kim, an educator of more years than she would like. They share a love for music and often perform together at church.

The Genesis of Creativity reflects his conviction that creativity is more than a skill, it's a calling rooted in the image of a creative God.

www.ingramcontent.com/pod-product-compliance
Lightning Source LLC
Chambersburg PA
CBHW022101090426
42743CB00008B/678